Leadership by Design

24 Intentional Actions to Inspire Great Leadership

ANNIE FRISOLI

LEADERSHIP BY DESIGN

24 INTENTIONAL ACTIONS TO INSPIRE GREAT LEADERSHIP

© 2024, Annie Frisoli.

Print ISBN: 979-8-35094-020-6
eBook ISBN: 979-8-35094-021-3

CONTENTS

INTRODUCTION

I believe people are our superpower.

S o much so that I felt compelled to write a book about it. I believe that when we dig deeper into what it means to be human, we can make positive, lasting contributions to our organizations, across our teams, within ourselves, and even to the world around us.

In an effort to help you invest in change by investing in yourself and your people, I've compiled some of my most valuable insights and impactful findings related to leadership, designing strong teams, inspiring our biggest assets (our people), and fostering a sense of belonging.

Driven by a desire to serve those who serve others, I've leveraged my experience as both a lifelong learner and multi-passionate leader to create this book. You might find it serves as a guide to help you prioritize mindfulness as a leader, cultivate greatness among your people, or look inward to strengthen your own values.

As you read on, you'll find helpful stories (both from myself and experts I trust), guidance to help you achieve harmony across teams, and thought-provoking topics to help you grow intentionally as a leader and person. My hope is that you'll walk away from this book with the confidence and mindset to implement a few of the insights that follow within your own organization, ultimately leading to healthier, happier, more effective teams.

Meet Annie (that's me)

If we haven't had the pleasure of meeting yet, hi, I'm Annie. You might be wondering where my insights and expertise come from, and the truth is, my background is a vibrant patchwork of unique experiences, energizing roles, and chance encounters with inspiring individuals.

To summarize my qualifications and experience here would be a challenge. If you ask me what makes me exceptionally qualified to help others grow into better leaders, I'd say it's my history of saying 'yes' to new opportunities, new people, and new experiences along my path. This trend has allowed me to collect uniquely valuable perspectives and insights over time.

Through it all, I've maintained a profound interest in developing a deeper understanding of the people around me. I've collected a network of insightful friends, family, and loved ones, and their incredible stories, which has enabled me to develop into the person I am today.

Aside from my experience as a partner, daughter, sister, best friend, adventurer, coach, and self-proclaimed "baking strategist," here are some of the more formal highlights along my path:

- Bachelor's degree from The University of Toledo in Therapeutic Recreation

- Master's degree from The University of North Carolina at Greensboro in Recreation Management

- Certified Festivals & Events Executive (CFEE)

- IFEA/NRPA Event Management School Instructor

- Certified in Foundations of Design Thinking

- Certified in Experience Innovation

- Certified Facilitator of Better Conversations Every Day™

- Certified Facilitator of the Center for Creative Leadership's Benchmarks® 360° Suite

- Certified Virtual Facilitator

- Multi-Award-Winning University Faculty Member

- Master Facilitator of Strategic Plans

- Master Facilitator of Designing THE Standard: Building Culture Within Your Organization

- Curriculum Designer for a Fortune 500 Company

- International-Level Conference Speaker and Trainer
  - More than 15,000 hours of facilitation

Now that we've met, let's dive in.

INSPIRING GROWTH BY DESIGNING BELONGING

This combination of words is what sparked the flame inside me that led to this book. If you're reading this, know that it means so much to me that you've chosen this book to help you dig a little deeper into what it means to be a leader.

To me, the phrase "inspiring growth by designing belonging" encapsulates the root of what I believe leadership should be. It means that by remaining intentional in our choices to foster connection across individuals and teams, we can stimulate happy, healthy, thriving organizations.

Putting this phrase into action requires a deeper understanding of each piece of the puzzle, which is why I've divided my insights into four sections. By cozying up to each individual component of this phrase, you can begin to make small adjustments that result in big changes - both in yourself and in others.

As you work through each section, keep in mind that my advice, guidance, and insights are just one perspective into the world around us. What's most important is that you take what serves you, and leave what doesn't. There isn't a one-size-fits-all approach to becoming a great leader, but I do believe that through small increments we can make a big impact on those around us.

Here's what each component of this golden phrase means to me:

- **Inspiring** others is our duty as leaders and people. To me, being "inspiring" is synonymous with being a facilitator of joy, motivation, drive, and development. As leaders, we have a responsibility to inspire good in others and set an example of what it means to thrive.

- **Growth** is the result of healthy inspiration and allows us to solidify skills that drive results. When we grow in the workplace, we're able to prioritize efficiency, success, our mission, and our goals, innovating along the way.

- **Designing** is an act done intentionally. Through careful consideration and mindfulness, we're able to use our influence to lead authentically by finding harmonious solutions to conflict and prioritizing balance across teams.

- **Belonging** makes us feel seen and heard, and results in healthier, happier people both at work and home. Of the many factors that contribute to a sense of belonging, I believe there are a few that can be prioritized to achieve better connectivity and a more meaningful purpose.

PART ONE:
INSPIRING

There's nothing quite as impactful as being told you've inspired someone else to take a leap, reach for more, or try something new. Maybe that's because we all know how critical it is to feel inspired along our paths to happiness and success. These points of inspiration often launch us into new, exciting chapters or the 'next big thing' in our journey, and when it strikes, we learn more about ourselves and what we're capable of.

The unique sense of euphoria that accompanies feeling inspired can be described as profoundly powerful. Magical. Kismet. Serendipitous. And to know that we've created that for others can feel equally as magnificent. As leaders, we have the opportunity to facilitate fearlessness and drive development in others.

Inspiring others doesn't (usually) happen by accident, though. And if our goal is to leave those we meet feeling inspired to reach for more, we must be intentional about how we support and motivate them.

In my own journey to become a better, more inspirational leader, I pay close attention to what works, and what doesn't. I quickly realized that while inspiration sometimes takes shape as electrically charged a-ha! moments (you know, the kind where someone says something that leaves their audience with goosebumps), it can also look like consistency, reliability, and quiet but fierce support.

If inspiring others was easy, we'd start every day with 5-minute inspirational stand-ups that send everybody back to their desks feeling like a million bucks. But since this isn't a realistic approach, we'll have to settle for gaining a better understanding of where inspiration comes from, how it works, and how we can harness more of it within our own organizations.

The first section of this book explores 'inspiration' as both a tool and an experience and should leave you feeling better equipped to create (and harness) inspiration across your interactions. If at any point you find yourself feeling inspired, give yourself the gift of jotting down a few notes somewhere to increase your chances of success and accountability. Also, I have created questions for reflection at the end of every chapter for you to think about individually, with your team, or you can even reach out to me, as I would love to connect!

1.
THE POWER OF AUTHENTICITY IN LEADERSHIP

"Real recognizes real. In order for people to trust and follow, you must give them your genuine self."
–Trevor Welcher, Parks & Recreation Director

You've probably noticed that inspiring others is both about what you say and what you do. Leadership exists in every moment, and while the occasional 'mic drop' moment can greatly impact a crowd or team meeting, these highly concentrated examples of inspiration are rare (and really difficult to replicate). Instead of trying to force eureka moments across teams or groups, I continue to return to what feels like the golden rule of leadership: leading by example.

There are several ways you've probably referred to this action-based approach to being an authentic leader:

- Practice what you preach.

- Put your money where your mouth is.

- Treat others how you want to be treated.

- Talk the talk, walk the walk.

- Lead by example.

All of these commonly used phrases nod to the power of using your actions to make an impact. Authenticity revolves around our actions and how we show up day in and day out, and since staying true to our own values is one of the greatest ways to promote a sense of authenticity at work, it's critical to prioritize consistency and reliability as a leader.

But why is authenticity such a catalyst for inspiration?

Authentic leaders have the ability to inspire employees to reach their full potential, and according to the Center for Creative Leadership[1], "Organizations that foster authentic leadership are more likely to have engaged, enthusiastic employees." When leaders show up consistently and authentically, they begin to build an atmosphere of transparency and unwavering trust, and when people see their leaders showing up as their true selves, they feel comfortable doing the same. The openness, honesty, and connection that result from this leadership style facilitate inspiration around every corner.

Empowering employees to embrace their own unique strengths, values, and skills starts with doing the same for ourselves. When we show up with confidence and embrace our individuality, we contribute to an environment that fosters this same sense of belonging. The result? Increased comfort levels at work, a deeper sense of community and connection, more creative thinking and collaboration, and a shared commitment to the bigger picture (aka your organization's mission, values, and goals).

Since showing up authentically is easier said than done, I've asked a few experts in my network to shed some light on how they work towards staying true to themselves at work and leveraging authenticity as a leader. Because contrary to popular belief, showing up authentically requires effort, especially for those of us who were told to soften some of our strongest qualities as we grew up. Here's what they said:

1. "When I was younger, I was very guarded in the workplace. What I realized however, is people couldn't get to know me, which meant I couldn't get to know them, and this ultimately made it more difficult to lead. I also realized, by not allowing people to know the authentic me, I allowed them to create a persona of me that most likely wasn't accurate. Over time, I have become more open and willing to be more vulnerable and authentic, and in return, people are more open with me, and we are able to form much richer relationships that positively impact the work we accomplish together." –Rosemary Richmond, Director of Customer Success

2. "There are so many pressures on you as a human being, not only in the workplace, but as a friend, parent, husband, sibling, mentor. That said, it is not always a simple task to be true to yourself. However,if you are authentic and make decisions based on who you are, your moral compass, and what you believe in – it becomes easier to cut through the noise and pressure. If you're genuine, you can lean on who you are, what you represent, and your morals. When those pressures do arrive, which are relentless, you don't have to continuously figure out how to address the particular issue or individual." –Stuart Schleien, Professor Emeritus, UNC Greensboro

3. "You can't lead everybody the same way. And so, if I want to be a person of influence and lead others, I have to know them, and

the way to get to know them is for them to know me." –Nathan Musteen, Director - Parks & Recreation, City of Raymore

4. "Authenticity is critical to being a leader. It normalizes that we're all humans who come to work each day, with life stories that are far bigger than the work we do. I've tended to see that people are more honest and trusting when they can show up as who they are and not try to hide parts of themselves. I see how much happier and open my students are when they feel like they can be themselves. When I show up as my silly self, it shows students that they can come to work as who they are and still put a good product or service forward." –Nicolette Griese, Assistant Director - Student Involvement Center, Fort Lewis College

These insights are a great reminder that there's no "right" way to show up authentically. The journey to authentic leadership will look different for everybody, especially since we each have unique strengths, qualities, and leadership styles.

Most importantly, remember that it isn't our job to be perfect. In fact, how we choose to show up in the face of imperfection says a whole lot more about who we are as leaders. While consistency is key, being truly authentic means acknowledging when consistency isn't possible, or when you missed the mark. Embracing every win, failure, and everything in between is a great way to prioritize authenticity at every turn, and empowering your team to do the same will help you take a collective step toward authenticity and connectivity together.

• •

Questions to reflect upon individually, with your team, or let's connect:

1. Why is authenticity such an important quality to harness as a leader?

2. How do you stay true to yourself, harness an authentic presence at work, and leverage the power of authenticity as a leader?

3. Can you share a specific example from your leadership experience where you felt being authentic had a positive impact on your team or organization?

4. What role does vulnerability play in authentic leadership, and how do you demonstrate vulnerability within your leadership style?

5. What practices do you have in place to help you stay self-aware and mindful of your authentic leadership style as you navigate challenges?

2.

INSPIRING OTHERS TO EXCEL

"Be THE standard."

–Bryan Dixon, Deputy Administrator,

Park Services, Henry County Parks and Recreation

I'm not very big on suggesting that there's only one way to achieve something, especially when it comes to leadership. The unique perspectives we bring to the table practically guarantee that we all approach leadership challenges differently, which conveniently allows us to learn by observing others approach common obstacles.

When exploring the topic of inspiring others, you'll find that there's a practically infinite number of ways to instill a sense of excitement and drive across teams. I couldn't possibly share a comprehensive snapshot of methods that have the potential to motivate your people, but I am eager to highlight some of my favorite tried-and-true methods of inspiring others.

Exploring what *doesn't* work.

Before we dive into a few examples of how to inspire others to excel, it's important to address what *doesn't* work. Because while there might be a million ways to approach a single challenge, my experience leading - and watching others lead - has revealed a few approaches that almost never work. In fact, certain actions can fail to inspire others and even leave them feeling defeated. Let's touch briefly on what to avoid if your goal is to nurture and support your team:

- **Giving employees less direction** can actually result in more confusion for them. While it might feel like a fresh or creative approach to leadership, teams thrive when they have just enough direction to feel confident in their decisions.

- **Overinvolved management styles** (also known as micromanaging) can have the opposite effect as intended. While it can be difficult to realize when we've wandered into micromanaging territory, a consistent desire for control and frequent critical feedback are likely signs that you're making things worse by over-involving yourself.

- **A lack of appreciation for employees** often results in a lack of effort on their part. When we forget to recognize the contributions of our teammates, we're telling our people that achievements don't matter or aren't worth celebrating.

  > Showing appreciation may seem like a simple suggestion, but it is more looked over than some would guess. When creating a strategic plan with a local parks and recreation agency, we surveyed approximately 70 full-time employees. One of the top-rated initiatives the team identified as they moved forward in their strategic growth was more recognition of the staff. They saw recognition as an opportunity to not only improve employee satisfaction but also feed into employee retention, which in turn impacts their ability to deliver services to the community. This is just one example

of how I have seen recognition and appreciation desired and prioritized by teams across the U.S.

- **Playing favorites among teammates** is a great way to discourage collaboration. While it might be tricky to find a balance between recognizing achievements and playing favorites, everyone must be recognized for their strengths without bias or favoritism.

Embracing what does work.

With your sights set on inspiring others to excel, it's important to remember not to overthink it. In my experience working with teams of all sizes across various industries, one thing is consistent - leaders often feel like they don't know where to start. They spend so much time trying to come up with new ways to inspire that they neglect to consider some of the more traditional, tried-and-true methods of motivation and inspiration. Some of my favorite approaches to inspiring people are simple, classic staples:

- **Leading by example** (as mentioned in the previous chapter) can help your team gain a better understanding of expectations and methods for success. Exemplify what it means to contribute, engage, and collaborate effectively, and watch your people do the same. Keep in mind that it's difficult to know when people are paying attention, which is why it's important to act as if every moment matters.

  As a former university faculty member, I've had numerous students reach back out years later and say, "I will never forget when you said or did…" Most of the time, I do not remember that moment, but it stands out to them as pivotal. Thus, we have to continually remind ourselves to lead by example and exude authenticity.

- **Encourage learning through failure** to boost the confidence of your people and avoid feelings of discouragement when things don't go as planned. We're only human, after all. Show your people that obstacles are opportunities to strengthen their skills and still come out on top.

- **Nurture inclusivity and positivity** to create an overarching sense of connection and respect among individuals. When your teams feel safe, they'll be more likely to contribute, speak up, and work towards shared goals as a team.

- **Facilitating autonomy and innovation** can give teams the spark they need to ignite their spirit. While it's important not to "let them loose" with no direction, allowing teams and individuals to explore new approaches or methods can instill a sense of confidence and drive.

- **When in doubt, ask your team** what motivates them. Leaders often take it upon themselves to have all the answers, neglecting to consider that their employees might have opinions about what they need, too. Resources like my Team Talk Cards (*anniefrisoli. com/teamtalkcards*) can make facilitating these conversations easier than ever.

I always recommend getting your people involved in their own development journey at work, welcoming them into "management style" conversations, and encouraging them to speak up if they have requests or notes for more efficient leadership. This way, leaders can adapt alongside colleagues to find a sense of harmony that results in thriving employees, teams, and organizations.

Many leaders and teams eventually settle into a rhythm, relying on the tactics that work best given their own unique circumstances. This can be a great way to provide consistent inspiration and give you something to fall back on when things aren't running as smoothly as usual. At the same time, try to avoid tunnel vision, and remain open to new opportunities for inspiration and motivation as they arise.

. . . .

Questions to reflect upon individually, with your team, or let's connect:

1. How do you show you appreciate others in the workplace? Could you be more intentional with showing appreciation?

2. In what ways do you encourage team members to share their preferences or feedback regarding the type of appreciation they find most meaningful?

3. What role does personalized recognition play in your appreciation strategy, and how do you ensure that it resonates with individual team members?

4. What creative or unique methods do you employ to express appreciation beyond traditional forms, such as verbal praise or recognition emails?

5. In what ways do you encourage peer-to-peer appreciation within the team, and how does this contribute to a positive workplace culture?

6. How do you ensure that appreciation is not just a one-time gesture but an ongoing part of the team culture?

3.
TURNING OBSTACLES INTO OPPORTUNITIES

"You will experience downfalls and shortcomings at some point in your life—how you recover from it will define who you are as a person."
–Trevor Welcher, Parks & Recreation Director

What if you could inspire your people long after they've logged off for the evening, or even while they're enjoying a weekend away from work? Sound too good to be true? This is another great example of how consistency with your actions and vocal support can result in a more consistent inspirational mindset, as opposed to short, fleeting bursts of motivation.

One way to strengthen this foundation for others is to help your teams achieve a mindset shift. If you aren't familiar, a mindset shift refers to the act of adjusting your perspective in order to approach it in a new, more productive way. As a leader, we help our people through mindset shifts like pessimism to optimism, features-to-benefits-focused, macro to micro thinking (or vice versa), and these shifts allow us to do our jobs better.

In my experience, one of the most rewarding mindset shifts that we can make is viewing obstacles as opportunities.

When acknowledging obstacles, many of us are immediately flooded with feelings of frustration, exhaustion, or sadness without even realizing it. If we can adapt our viewpoint to minimize negative reactions and instead focus on the opportunities in front of us, or harness feelings of motivation, we can maintain a more confident, inspired outlook at work, at home, and beyond.

Shifting towards a more resourceful, optimistic mindset in the face of obstacles requires us to unlearn many of the habits we've built to protect ourselves, or simply just grown accustomed to. But immediate dread and pessimism in the face of a challenge is not sustainable, and only leaves us feeling defeated before we've even had a chance to consider solutions.

One of the ways I support people on their journey to unlearn this frustration reflex is to remind them of the obstacles in our past that led to big wins or successes. When we reflect on the challenges that facilitated more fun, a deeper understanding, creative breakthroughs, and success, we can eventually develop a less defensive attitude toward difficult tasks.

But as leaders, we can do more than help our teams unlearn the habit of reacting negatively to challenges, we can also introduce new habits that further strengthen their ability to approach problems with grit and grace. Some of my favorite ways to inspire a greater sense of confidence in teams include:

- Communicating early about the resources and guidance that will be available to teams in the face of this new challenge. This helps them feel supported and prepared.

- Reassuring them that there's no right way to solve this problem (if applicable). Encouraging out-of-the-box thinking reminds them that there are no wrong answers.

- Leading by example by getting in on the action and participating in brainstorming sessions or ideation meetings. This helps set the tone and lets everybody skip through that awkward "what do we do now?" stage.

- Recognizing small wins and contributions to inspire more collaboration and creativity. This adds positive milestones to the process of tackling the latest challenge, negating some stress and frustration.

- Allowing space and time for team members to express their fears while encouraging them not to dwell. By creating this space, you can help them process negative thoughts quicker and in good company, supporting their positive mindset. - Check out the Build, Barrier & Beyond template at *anniefrisoli.com* to facilitate a conversation around both fears and forward thought process.

- Reminding teams about the bigger picture, mission, or company-wide goals can motivate teams towards a deeper purpose and nurture their sense of belonging.

By implementing any of these strategies, you can help your teams reframe their approach to problem-solving in the face of new or intimidating challenges. Through consistent practice, repetition, and reflection, we can *all* learn to adopt a more inspired mindset, essentially teaching our brain that obstacles are merely opportunities for greatness in disguise.

Remember when I asked how it would feel to know you could inspire others during their time away from work? This mindset shift doesn't only impact the work your employees do, it also impacts how they view the world. Instilling them with a sense of self-assuredness means that they can spend less time getting in their own way, and more time approaching life from a more elevated, open perspective. This ultimately results in more efficient and effective creative thinking, allowing us to embrace new approaches with enthusiasm and joy.

Don't be surprised if, over time and with practice, your teams develop a zest for challenges and an eagerness to share their own 'aha!' moments with others on Monday mornings or via email after hours.

• •

Questions to reflect upon individually, with your team, or let's connect:

1. *Challenge:* Spend one day listening/noticing how others respond in conversation. Do they tend to have a negative or positive response to topics being shared? How can you reframe some of the negative mindsets? How can you continue to encourage positive responses?

2. What is an obstacle you and your team have overcome? How can you leverage this example to inspire them in any current or future challenges?

3. How do you handle resistance or skepticism from team members when implementing solutions to overcome obstacles?

4. What steps do you take to ensure that the solutions implemented to overcome obstacles are sustainable in the long term?

5. How do you communicate the importance of learning from obstacles rather than viewing them solely as setbacks?

4.

LEADING WITH CLARITY THROUGH EFFECTIVE COMMUNICATION

"If we are unable to communicate,
we will not grow or succeed."
—Ed Stuczynski—aka Eddie

C larity is key. Clarity is kind. Clarity is king (or queen). There's a reason we've found so many ways to give 'clarity' the hype it deserves, and it's because, without it, life tends to feel chaotic. Clarity is such an important component of leadership because it's what allows us to quickly distribute information, connect deeply with our teams, and collaborate more effectively. But earning the right to say you prioritize clarity as a leader isn't as easy as noting "My door is always open," or "I'm an open book." To inject clarity into your organization, you have to consciously communicate in a way that your teams can quickly digest and execute.

Throughout more than 15,000 hours of facilitation and training, I've continued to observe reminders that effective communication is one of the most powerful vehicles for increasing clarity at work. It might seem obvious, or not worth mentioning, but here's why it's so important...

Many leaders think that clarity will follow suit if they err on the side of over-communicating. The hope behind this mindset is that the more you say, the more they'll understand, but this approach neglects to prioritize efficiency or effectiveness in communication. Instead, it prioritizes quantity over quality, resulting in less clarity and more confusion for all.

So how can we prioritize quality over quantity when it comes to communication?

How can we slow down enough to remain intentional and clear without info-dumping on our people and overwhelming them with details?

How can we keep them involved without asking them to carry the weight of our own roles?

Based on my experience as a leader, facilitator, and consultant, I'm eager to highlight a few insights that might help you master your communication skills and prioritize clarity within your own organization:

- **Do the prep work ahead of big conversations or new projects**. Taking time to process and review the information you're about to share (a new project, an upcoming change, a not-so-fun announce-ment) can help you identify which pieces of the puzzle will be useful to your team (and which might be unnecessary to share). Consider the questions that might arise and your team's capacity for additional tasks or input, and dial in your conversation ahead of time. Practicing your delivery can help you avoid overloading them with needless mental clutter. You can find another useful template, Connecting With Purpose, on my website *anniefrisoli. com,* to assist you in your preparation.

- **Practice active listening**. True active listening will ensure you don't miss requests, questions, and opportunities for more clarity.

In addition to listening with your ears, don't forget to look for visual clues that signal feelings of overwhelm, confusion, or concern. Sometimes, opportunities for increased clarity are easy to spot on the faces you've grown familiar with. You can learn more about testing and sharpening your team's listening skills through my staff development training - Communication by Design - on my website (*anniefrisoli.com*).

- **Cut down on ambiguity**. While acronyms or jargon might be commonplace in your industry or organization, they can sometimes do more harm than good. To minimize inefficiencies, work on communicating with straightforward, direct language to outline timelines, objectives, and tasks. Along the same vein, it's important to avoid assumptions (you know what they say).

- **Remain consistent in your communication style**. Some organizations or teams leverage tools like email, Slack, Teams, SMS, intranet, CRMs, or other messaging software to keep in touch. While this approach has several benefits, it can also lead to a lack of clarity if messaging across platforms isn't consistent, or if communication happens across far too many channels. Align your messaging across communication methods to make sure nothing is missed or misconstrued.

- **Distribute updates with transparency and authenticity**. Create communication plans that go along with the work, don't risk new ideas or updates being unsuccessful due to poor communication. When your people can rely on you to keep them in the loop, you'll probably notice a significant decrease in the number of questions, insecurities, and concerns that arise. Building a solid foundation of trust through active communication in this way will contribute to calm, clear minds.

If your goal is to create a culture rooted in clarity, knowing how to communicate clearly is a must. And on your journey to prioritizing efficiency and effectiveness in your communication style, remember that nobody masters it overnight. Focusing on one area of improvement at a time can help you make small-but-mighty shifts across your teams, forming better communication habits across the board.

• •

Questions to reflect upon individually, with your team, or let's connect:

1. Do you have strategies or an identified communication plan to cascade information to your team, across divisions, throughout the organization, to those outside the organization?

2. Do those that need to be involved in the dissemination of information have clarity on the information and how it should be disseminated?

3. How do you tailor your communication style to accommodate the diverse preferences and needs of team members?

4. In what ways do you measure the effectiveness of your communication, and how do you gather feedback from team members regarding the clarity of your messages?

5. How do you ensure that communication remains two-way, with ample opportunities for team members to provide input and ask questions?

5.

EMBRACING THE UNKNOWN: NAVIGATING UNCERTAINTY WITH CONFIDENCE

"You have to practice being a leader."

–Patrick Hammer, Director of Parks and Recreation, Town of Erie

You'd be hard-pressed to find a leader - or anyone, for that matter - willing to take on *more* uncertainty in their role. And yet, uncertainty throughout projects, collaborative efforts, and even organization-wide missions is inevitable. Since we can't predict the future (at least...I sure can't) and haven't yet found a way to solve problems instantaneously, uncertainty is just a part of life that we all must navigate daily.

If you've ever been faced with an unexpected detour on your route (literally OR metaphorically), been assigned a new project or task without warning, encountered a seemingly impossible challenge, or simply found yourself surprised by something in your path, you've undoubtedly overcome uncertainty. You made it to your destination, tackled or delegated that project, and found a way to address surprises or concerns. Perhaps it was successful, or maybe it served as a learning experience, but either way, you were able to navigate the uncertainty. Was it calm and comfortable or stressful and anxiety-inducing? And how can you set yourself up for the former instead of the latter?

Embracing the unknown to navigate uncertainty with *confidence* is crucial to effective leadership, especially since it sets the tone for your people to do the same. The reality of our work today is dynamic and unpredictable, so being able to respond with comfort, clarity, and ease - instead of uncertainty, anxiety, or overwhelm - is key.

One of the best ways to strengthen your self-confidence in the face of uncertainty is to cozy up to what *uncertainty* really means for you and where it comes from. Uncertainty arises for several reasons - things like technological advancements and innovation, market trends or expansion, or global events (remember 2020?) can all have an impact on the level of uncertainty baked into our roles and everyday lives.

When and how it shows up may differ, feeling like unanswered questions, an opportunity for curiosity, or a general lack of confidence in the tasks at hand. It involves not knowing what to do next, feeling stuck, or being caught off guard by an obstacle in your path. While these descriptions might sound vague, the truth is that uncertainty feels different for everyone, but you'll likely feel it when it arrives. The same is true for your people, so it's important to keep in mind that what feels like uncertainty to you might be a whole lot different than how they perceive uncertainty.

The most important first step in facing uncertainty with clarity and confidence is adopting the mindset shift I mentioned in Chapter 3. If you can learn to see obstacles as opportunities, your relationship with uncertainty will feel much more relaxed, and maybe even energizing.

In addition to this mindset shift, building resilience in your teams can help them maintain their composure in the face of ongoing obstacles or sudden challenges. We'll talk more about building resiliency in part two of this book.

There are a few tried-and-true ways that I've been able to help teams and leaders strategically face uncertainty and overcome it with ease, including:

- Increased self-awareness and emotional intelligence through 360° feedback.

   ◦ This can help maintain confidence across groups and results in smoother transitions into problem-solving mode. As a 360° Certified Facilitator of the Center for Creative Leadership's Benchmarks® 360° Suite, I have seen first hand how this type of feedback can grow self-awareness.

- Fostering adaptability and lifelong learning.

   ◦ Embracing the fact that we're all constantly facing new obstacles and uncertainty can help bolster comradery and introduce a sense of acceptance.

- Embracing failure or uncertainty as an opportunity for growth.

   ◦ Shifting the way we look at uncertainty can lead to learning opportunities and fresh perspectives, allowing teams to grow alongside each other.

- Establishing support networks across teams.

   Helping your people establish mentorships and support systems will give them someone to lean on in times of uncertainty, stress, and opportunity.

As you work towards helping your team embrace uncertainty in their path, you may notice that they struggle to make decisions or decide what to do next. Sometimes, uncertainty causes us to freeze or stumble instead of marching on. As a leader, you have an opportunity to guide people through these moments and coach them on how to brainstorm to find the next steps, take breaks to clear their heads, or work together to find new solutions.

This guidance can help inspire your team before, during, and after uncertainty strikes, and will eventually enable them to strengthen their self-confidence and begin tackling uncertainty with ease. Along the way, you can further support them by providing a clear vision and purpose, maintaining efficient communication, remaining an empowering and supportive ally, and modeling resilience along the way.

Several blog posts on my website (*anniefrisoli.com*) include tangible tips surrounding embracing the unknown and trying new things, including:

- Be The Weakest Performer: Leadership Tips From The Gym

- "Where's The Shovel? - How Seeking New Experiences Makes You A More Agile Leader

• •

Questions to reflect upon individually, with your team, or let's connect:

1. Can you share an example from your experience where embracing uncertainty led to positive outcomes or innovative solutions within your team or organization?

2. Have you ever participated in a 360° feedback process? If you did, what did you learn? If you have not, how could a process like this be helpful to you as a professional?

3. How do you manage the potential anxiety or resistance that may arise among team members during uncertain times, and how does this impact your leadership approach?

4. In what ways do you involve the team in decision-making processes during periods of uncertainty to foster a sense of ownership and collective responsibility?

5. What role does continuous learning and professional development play in building resilience and adaptability within your team during uncertain times?

6.

MOTIVATING "STUCK" TEAMS

"Balancing attention between your team and achieving goals is pivotal. A successful team can drive the work forward, yet your presence and support are essential for them to excel and achieve the overall strategic objectives."
–Joseph Stuczynski, PMP, CSM

If you've been leading teams for a while, you've more than likely encountered at least one group that seems to be stuck in a state of inaction or underperformance. "Stuck" teams might present as unmotivated, unwilling to attack a challenge with gusto, or even burnt out and tired at work. In cases like these, motivating a group into an active, participatory state requires more than friendly competition, polite asks, or small incentives.

Observing teams who struggle to reach their full potential can be hard on the heart. As passionate leaders, seeing people work together but not *work* together can be difficult to digest. But before we jump in to motivate them with a pep talk or attempt to appeal to their inner creative genius, it's important to step back to get the full picture and create an intentional plan of attack to inspire them to reach for more.

When we begin by attempting to understand the underlying causes for this sense of "stuck" across a team or individual, we're one step closer to finding the most appropriate and effective solution. As part of the assessment phase, I find it helps to look for factors like unclear or conflicting goals, a lack of opportunities for growth, challenges, or promotion, gaps in communication from leadership or team members, or even personal issues that may be unknown. All of these factors can impact the way a person shows up to work, and each factor will require a unique approach tailored to that individual, the organization, and their current challenges. I love working with teams to use the Direction, Alignment, and Commitment Assessment[2] developed by the Center for Creative Leadership, which can be found on their website and is included in the Sources and Citations section at the end of this book.

Once you've taken the time to understand what's going on for specific team members or teams as a whole, it's time to motivate toward a purpose. By reconnecting employees with both their sense of purpose and a shared sense of purpose across the team or organization, you might find that inspiration and their spark returns quickly (though, sometimes, good things just take time). I like to help people reconnect with their purpose through informal and collaborative conversations about what drives us (and why), and communicating the value that each individual brings to the team, the organization, and my life personally. These tactics go a long way in helping people better understand the significance behind the work that they do.

In my experience, a good next step is to work on developing a growth mindset like we've talked about in previous chapters and will talk even more about in part two. This involves shifting their perspective in the face of challenges to see through a more optimistic lens, harnessing the opportunities presented to them instead of becoming discouraged by obstacles. Later on, we'll break this approach down even further so you can master it for yourself.

After you've successfully inspired a growth mindset in your people, it's time to set clear - and challenging - goals to get them fired up and ready to re-engage with their work. After several years of helping leaders and teams set goals for themselves, here are my top tips for making sure your goals are solid enough to motivate and inspire action:

- **Make them measurable (don't just let them be pretty).** Immeasurable goals deprive people of feeling they've succeeded, achieved, or beat expectations.

- **Clarity is key.** Goals should be well outlined, thoroughly explained, and understood by all before getting started to eliminate inefficiencies and miscommunications.

- **Give them a challenge.** Easy goals might be perceived as pandering or even insulting, but challenging goals can inspire action and give them something rewarding to work toward.

- **Invite them to participate.** Get them involved in goal-setting to introduce a sense of ownership and commitment to the challenge.

- **Break things down.** Identifying smaller milestones will increase opportunities for check-ins, celebrations, and recognition of wins to boost morale and excitement.

One of my favorite ways to approach the final two steps mentioned above is to empower and delegate with care. By delegating in a way that allows team members to shine in their areas of expertise or interest, especially outside of their traditional list of duties, you're inviting more creative energy, self-expression, and freedom into the equation. When people feel like they have an opportunity to showcase their skills and talents (while still being supported and encouraged), they're more likely to show up for the challenge.

Acknowledging these efforts and triumphs further enforces the hard work and dedication that they've shown, inspiring them to strive for more.

Once your clear, creative, and challenging goals have been set and your team feels adequately empowered, it's time to celebrate. With feedback and recognition, of course! This can (and should) happen on both an individual and team level to acknowledge improvements and achievements for all. By celebrating milestones of all sizes and identifying areas where more support may be needed, you're reminding them that they always have someone in their corner willing to back them up and cheer them on, and who doesn't love that feeling?

Finally, don't forget to lead by example. As their leader, motivator, and champion, you're uniquely positioned to set the tone for how and when people can dig in and reach for more at work. Your enthusiasm and dedication to the cause can be combined with a willingness to "get your hands dirty," resulting in a team that feels more comfortable getting started and more comforted by a supportive presence. It's in these moments that our passion as leaders can ignite a spark in our people and inspire them to show up with unwavering confidence and drive.

· ·

Questions to reflect upon individually, with your team, or let's connect:

1. How do you identify and diagnose the specific challenges that are causing a team to feel "stuck"?

2. How do YOU stay motivated when you or the team is feeling stuck?

3. How often do you revisit individual and team goals with those you lead to assist with overcoming the feeling of being stuck?

4. What steps do you take to assess and address team dynamics and communication issues that may contribute to a feeling of being stuck?

5. If you are dealing with a stuck team, what is one intentional move you will try for the next five days to start to move the team forward?

PART TWO:
GROWTH

O bserving others grow, blossom, and thrive under your leadership is a special kind of thrill. When you finally see someone take that leap, embrace their challenges head-on, or step into their full potential, it feels exhilarating and likely leaves you with an electric sense of awe.

Whether you've been doing this for a few days or a few decades, seeing your efforts make a tangible impact on others is profoundly satisfying. As leaders, we're tasked with the responsibility - and given the opportunity - to cultivate an environment of growth, support, and innovation. When it finally happens, we're reminded of the importance of these responsibilities.

Unlocking the growth potential within ourselves and those we lead takes more than a little faith, trust, and pixie dust. But once we collect the right tools in our leadership toolbox and feel confidently equipped to foster growth in others, we can cultivate greatness across our organization in a way that is both sustainable and powerful.

To become better leaders and inspire growth in others, we have to embark on our own self-improvement journey to embrace an eager, curious mindset. Being open to new ideas, fresh perspectives, and even quirky tactics can open new doors for possibility within ourselves, our teams, and our organization. Once we've accepted our role as lifelong learners, we can begin to inspire others to do the same.

Early on in my leadership journey, I experienced this realization firsthand. It became apparent that everything I knew about leadership and inspiring growth wasn't working with the people I'd taken under my wings. Instead of continuing to try the same approach with the hopes that something would change, I finally looked inward to explore what else *I* could learn. The answer? A lot. I learned new things about the people in my network and on my teams, new tactics for fostering growth, and new ways of communicating my message.

But what kind of self-exploration and learning does it take to become a leader who fosters growth in people, and cultivates supportive, empowering environments? Ask 100 successful leaders and you'd get 100 different answers, but I'm willing to bet that these answers have a few common themes. In this section of the book, we're breaking down some of these common themes and providing realistic, tangible tactics you can explore to help inspire growth in yourself and across teams.

7.

THE POWER OF CURIOSITY: CULTIVATING A CULTURE OF CONTINUOUS LEARNING

*"Curiosity is a skill set and
it's a skill that has to be developed."*

—Bernita, Director

C uriosity is one of my all-time favorite qualities to help leaders develop in their teams. Not only does it serve as a catalyst for growth and innovation across organizations, but it also boosts morale and increases collaborative efforts for all. If you ask me, there's nothing that a little curiosity can't solve, so I'm passionate about emphasizing the role that we play as leaders in fostering a culture that values and promotes continuous learning through curiosity.

I've been lucky enough to observe the impact that a little extra curiosity can have on high-performing teams, stuck teams, and every kind of team in between. In fact, my curiosity skills have been developed intentionally by some of the incredible leaders and connections along my journey, sharpening my ability to problem solve, innovate, and think outside of the box. Here are some of my favorite curiosity-based tips and insights straight from my network of curious leaders:

1. "To me, [curiosity] is about coaching and developing. I coach and develop with a mindset of letting the person you are leading guide you with *their* level of comfort vs. guiding them on *your* level of comfort. Some leaders don't allow for curiosity, they just tell their people how to do things [instead of] leading them to their own curiosity. Letting people be curious and know they don't have to do the job the exact same way you would is important. It's asking questions and then sitting back to allow them to be curious as to how they will complete the goal. Leadership is a lot about guiding them towards their own abilities and decisions, it's not necessarily giving them the direction that they need to flow in." –Bernita, Director

2. "Being brave enough to share [your] ideas with others and allowing them to poke holes in your thoughts is when you know that you are growing and secure enough with yourself to let others see your true self. In order to grow, we must fail, or we will never get better." –Nancy Pfeffer, Regional Manager, CPRP, The Maryland - National Capital Park and Planning Commission

3. "Without curiosity, there is no drive for learning, which can result in complacency. Offering new project opportunities allows for professional development experiences which can be highlighted at annual reviews and on resumes for future positions. All of these experiences perpetuate growth, which naturally leads to a collaborative environment." –Jennifer Kempert, Recreation & Special Events Coordinator

4. "When people approach new ideas with negativity, I try to lean in and be curious as to whether or not their negativity towards the new idea is valid or maybe they just want to be heard. Once I hear their response, I can better respond to their resistance. I also feel barriers to curiosity may be more of a sign of how frantic or unorganized a person is feeling in their current work. If this is the case, then again, I can better respond to the situation." –Patrick Hammer, Director of Parks and Recreation, Town of Erie

When it comes to nurturing the curiosity of others, we can start by emphasizing the sheer value of curiosity - both at work and at home. Most people think curiosity is all about asking more questions, and they're not wrong. Being comfortable and willing to ask questions that feel mold-breaking or unusual is a great skill to develop, and will undoubtedly result in an improved approach to problem-solving. Here are a few of my go-to questions to help inspire new ideas and fresh approaches:

- What are you afraid of in this situation?

- What difference do you want to make?

- If you had a genie in a bottle and could make a wish, what would you ask for?

- If there were no time, money, or staff constraints, how would you resolve this issue?

- If we had nothing to lose, how would you go about solving this problem?

In addition to asking more questions, though, curiosity also shows up as an independent willingness to try new things and explore unique solutions. When our people are at their desks and focused on their tasks and projects, are they going through the motions, or are they seeking out fresh opportunities and unique approaches to challenges and goals? This is the difference between a lack and a surplus of curious thinking.

Instead of settling for the mindset of "we've always done it this way," curious team members often find ways to maximize their own efficiency and enjoyment at work. As my good friend and speaker, author, and podcaster Anthony Iracki notes on his blog[3], one of the greatest swaps we can make for this stifling phrase is "let's try that again."

In turn, this mindset shift results in the introduction of new processes or innovative procedures that can be shared across teams, contributing to the growth of our organizations over time.

We can also thank curious team members for contributing to the flow of ideas and collaboration during meetings or brainstorms, asking questions that others may be too shy to ask, and bringing a healthy dose of creative energy to the culture and atmosphere of our organizations. When curiosity and creativity flow freely throughout our teams, everybody wins.

In order to fuel a culture of continuous learning and curiosity, we can continually introduce opportunities for our people to flex their curious mindset, and nurture this curiosity through patience and support. Creating an environment free of judgment, shame, and unhealthy criticism is key to helping curiosity blossom. When people feel it's safe to *not* know the answer, they feel comfortable being outwardly curious and explorative in their roles.

I like to introduce opportunities for teams to be curious together as a way of getting them more comfortable with uncertainty and the unknown. Rewarding people for asking questions, introducing new ideas, and putting their creativity on display can be a great way to support, nurture, and model continuous learning and a creative mindset.

Leading by example is another great way to help your people cozy up to their own curiosity. By modeling a curious mindset, you're reinforcing the idea that it's okay not to know the answers and that exploring your options through creative thinking is both productive and fruitful. For some, it's easy to forget that leaders, especially their own, are also on a journey of self-improvement. We're in a unique position to remind our people that learning never stops, and in fact, when it does, so does productivity and growth.

Curiosity is often a product of its environment. When group interaction is facilitated, playfulness is encouraged, and questions are accepted without judgment, curiosity blossoms. An emphasis on collaboration and connection allows everyone to get involved and feed off of each other's energy and curiosity.

Another great way to cultivate a culture rooted in continuous learning is to encourage frequent exploration of new skills, tasks, and even hobbies. A playful approach to professional development can ignite the spark within people, leading them to discover interests they didn't know they had, or talents they didn't know they were eager to develop. Instead of encouraging your teams to develop skills that already exist, challenge them to think outside of the box to explore something new. As a bonus, introducing new growth opportunities can be a great way to reduce boredom at work and keep your people engaged.

Don't forget that you can foster collaboration and knowledge sharing within *and* between your people. Curious and creative mindsets are incredibly valuable, but this value grows exponentially when they're combined through collaboration. It's one thing to help individuals develop their own curiosity, and it's another to help them combine and compound this curiosity with others. With practice and over time, your people will begin to feel comfortable taking advantage of opportunities to let their curiosity shine, opening the door for others to tap in with ideas and insights. Through opportunities like these, we can all learn from each other's findings, successes, and failures to create highly informed and effective teams.

By supporting your team on their path to explore new ideas, take calculated risks, and learn from their mistakes, you're reinforcing the idea that good things come from being curious and open to lifelong learning. If your mission is to stay ahead, drive innovation, and unlock the potential of your people, curiosity will take you there.

· ·

Questions to reflect upon individually, with your team, or let's connect:

1. How do you stay curious in your own role?

2. What factors (both internal and external) prevent you from staying curious in your role?

3. What role does curiosity play when attempting to cultivate growth among your people? As a leader, how can you encourage and reward curiosity?

4. How has curiosity benefitted you, your team, and/or your organization?

8.

EMPOWERING AND ENABLING GROWTH AND RESILIENCY

"Without resilience, life will run you over."
–Judd Walker, Director of Student Leadership, Ohio University

I f long-term success and the ability to overcome challenges are on your list of goals for your team, helping your people harness resiliency and a growth mindset are two effective ways you can get there.

As leaders, we're given the opportunity to empower and enable growth and resiliency within our teams, something I find essential for gracefully and efficiently achieving collective goals. But instilling resilience and growth mindsets requires patience and consistency on your part as a leader, and in a world where you likely don't need (or want) to add *another* thing to your plate, I'm on a mission to simplify the process.

By curating an environment that supports both personal and professional development, I believe that you can inspire your teams to reach their full potential while adapting to changing circumstances. This sense of resiliency and grit through times of change will lead to stronger, healthier, happier teams within your organization. Here are some suggestions:

1. **Set a clear vision and goals.**

    As a leader, you're tasked with the job of providing a clear vision and setting meaningful, measurable goals that align with your organization's mission. By communicating this vision to your team, you can ensure that everyone has a solid understanding of their role in achieving it. Clarity of purpose and direction enables your people to focus their efforts and work collaboratively towards these shared objectives.

2. **Leverage open and transparent communication.**

    By establishing open lines of communication, you're one step closer to creating an empowering environment for your team. Encourage your team members to share ideas, concerns, questions, and feedback whenever it arises - or during designated times - to further emphasize your openness and availability as a leader, as well as the safety of your team. By actively listening to their input and providing constructive, supportive feedback, you can create an environment that feels secure for all. Remain transparent about decisions that affect your team to build trust and foster growth.

3. **Effectively delegate and enable autonomy.**

    When we delegate responsibilities, we grant our teams autonomy over their work, bolstering their sense of independence. By allowing our teams to make decisions and solve problems, they're able to take ownership of their tasks and work, which leads to increased creativity, builds confidence, and even allows them to develop new skills and strengths.

"I do my best to offer support and then get out of their way! People learn by "doing" much better than they learn by being told. I believe the best leaders surround themselves with strong, skilled, authentic people and support them while they do their thing! I also think that we can sometimes overuse the phrase, "learn from mistakes," but the reality is that it is an accurate sentiment and is one of the top ways to establish resiliency among your team." - Mairin Petrone, Executive Director, Pittsburgh Irish Festival

4. **Lean into continuous learning and development.**
    In the previous chapter, I covered several of the benefits of fostering curiosity and continuous learning, including the exponential growth of your people's skill sets. You can support a curious culture within your teams by encouraging them to expand their knowledge and skills through workshops, mentorship, or other professional development outlets. By providing resources and opportunities for growth, you can recognize achievements and encourage the evolution of your people. And one of my top ideas is to host professional development workshops for your team and have them collectively learn together on topics related to communication, innovation, team development, and leadership - you will be amazed at all the wonderful conversations and ideas that emerge from this experience. One of my favorite designs was working collaboratively with a team to host their own Leadership Summit. Instead of only sending a select few to a conference or training, this design allowed for all team members to participate in professional development.

5. **Prioritize constructive feedback and coaching.**
    You can regularly provide effective feedback to help your team members grow and strengthen their resiliency. By offering praise

and recognition for their achievements while simultaneously guiding in areas where they can benefit, you're able to instill more passion and the ability to bounce back from challenges, mistakes, or failures.

6. **Normalize collaboration and teamwork.**

   Fostering and embracing a collaborative environment where everyone learns from each other, shares ideas, and works together towards common goals is a little bit like being insured against discouragement and burnout in times of change. When teamwork and collaboration are normalized and embraced, your team can rely on each other for camaraderie and connectivity. This also helps them feel safer and more comfortable when things get difficult, and benefit from each other's insights to work more efficiently and effectively.

7. **Instill adaptability and resilience.**

   You can demonstrate adaptability and resilience in the face of change and adversity to exemplify what it means to navigate a storm and come out on top. By emphasizing the importance of embracing challenges and learning from failures, you can inspire your team to bounce back from obstacles feeling stronger than ever. This encouragement can help your team view setbacks as learning opportunities while providing a comprehensive sense of support.

   > "Adaptability is a common denominator of people and organizations who remain effective and relevant over decades." –Mark Black in *The Resilience Roadmap: 7 Guideposts for Charting Your Course in a Chaotic World*[5]

"I don't know that I empower and enable [growth and resiliency] as much as I try to be the example of it. I think by being the example, you enable other people to grow because they see you continue to show up, stay positive in challenging situations, and do the hard work. You don't just show them when you're tough to enable resiliency, you show them your weaknesses and insecurities too." –Nathan Musteen, Director - Parks & Recreation, City of Raymore

"Resilience is an important quality because [work] is cyclical. Sometimes, things are good, registration is good, then a class doesn't run, or people want something new. Drawing on your experience and knowledge, resilience will help you pivot and find a new direction to get things back on track." –Maria C. Klein, Art Department Coordinator

8. **Encourage recognition and empathy.**
While nurturing your team's sense of grit is important, it's equally important to remember that it's okay not to function at extraordinarily high levels every day. In fact, this can lead to burnout and detachment from work. Instead, find a balance between encouragement of strong qualities like growth and resilience while also nurturing qualities like empathy and support. By prioritizing this sense of balance, you'll find a healthy medium of enthusiasm for work and an understanding that sometimes, we aren't performing at our best. Recognition for success is great, but success isn't always the outcome, so recognition of someone's qualities and valuable traits can be a fantastic way to support people through life's ups and downs.

Reflecting on this list of 8 methods for empowering growth and resiliency, I can't help but think of it as a great generalized checklist of what good leadership looks like. By prioritizing these aspects at work, you'll be empowering and enabling dozens of great qualities for your people, and the trust, support, and collaboration that follows is just the cherry on top.

• •

Questions to reflect upon individually, with your team, or let's connect:

1. How do you empower and enable growth and resiliency as a leader?

2. What small-but-mighty tactics do you rely on to help nurture qualities like growth and resilience?

3. Why is a sense of resilience so important for individuals to possess?

4. What role do team development strategies or workshops play in strengthening relationships and resilience within your team?

5. What role does team empowerment play in your approach to building resilience, and how do you foster a sense of ownership among team members?

9.
LEVERAGING THE DIGITAL AGE
TO INSTILL GROWTH

"Nothing you learn is ever wasted."
–Christine Frisoli, aka Mom

While it might not always feel like modern technology is something to be thankful for, as leaders, we're actually quite privileged to have so many incredible tools at our disposal. Despite the technical difficulties and forgotten passwords and software updates (oh my!), the digital age has opened doors that previously didn't exist. The truth is, our ability to lead can be made easier and more convenient through modern technology if only we know how to harness it.

In fact, by leveraging some of these tools effectively, we can increase communication, efficiency, influence, and even accessibility across our teams. Don't let apps, social networks, or trending software scare you - keeping up with your people doesn't have to feel like a chore. Getting involved in modern digital tools can actually serve as a collaborative learning (and bonding) experience, all while maximizing efficiency or enjoyment in the workplace.

Aside from some of the more obvious tools of the digital age (like email or cloud storage), there are a few ways I've seen effective leaders leverage modern technology to extend their reach and make an impact within and beyond their own organizations. In an effort to inspire you to try something new and harness the power of the digital age, I'm sharing a few of these findings and some of my own here:

- **Data Analysis for Decision-Making**

  There are several modern and emerging software options and solutions that exist to help you analyze, visualize, and share your team's data. Whether you're hoping to monitor your team's output, effectiveness, efficiency, collaborative success, or something else entirely, taking advantage of high-powered tools can help you do it. An excellent blog post from IDEO U[6] includes several great examples and notes that, "Instead of immediately optimizing for numbers like revenue and engagement, ask the why behind the problem." Imagine what you and your teams could change or improve if you knew which tasks took up the most unnecessary time, which meetings resulted in the least productivity, or which team members collaborated the most effectively. Leaders willing to take advantage of tools that track and produce data are then able to share results with their teams, clients, or even consumers to make an even bigger impact.

- **Social Media and Online Presence**

  If you happen to work with a group that is commonly online or prioritizes a social presence, it might be worth your while to find a way to engage with them in this space. Now, this doesn't necessarily mean you should follow all of your team members on Instagram (unless that feels like the right approach). Instead, ask yourself if you can foster a more connected community on LinkedIn or through a shared Facebook group (you can find mine here: *facebook.com/groups/weinspirecommunity*) to increase the opportunity for interaction in a casual way. Maybe this means celebrating promotions with "likes" on their LinkedIn post or having people vote on the next caterer for the upcoming Lunch & Learn via a Facebook poll or hosting a Pop Up Singalong and posting the group video online to spread joy to others or hosting a giveaway and choosing the winner on a LIVE social media platform. Having conversations outside of a typical work environment can create a better sense of camaraderie and connectivity.

- **Accommodations for Accessibility**
  In a world where so much technology exists, there are a practically infinite number of ways we can support and accommodate our people and their needs. Team members struggling with physical disabilities, neurodivergence, or other challenges can benefit greatly from various tools, software, apps, and accommodations that result from living in a high-tech world. Creating space and openness for employees to independently harness the power of digital solutions (like time-tracking tools, visual or auditory aids, or ergonomic technology) can help create a more comfortable and efficient environment for your teams. The ability to meet our people where they're at is a tremendous benefit of life in the 21st century. If your organization frequently plans events or in-person activities, visit *everyonesinvited.com* for resources and inspiration to help prioritize accessibility.

- **Personal Development and Interests**
  In the modern world, personal development doesn't always look like in-person conferences or courses at the local university. In fact, as a result of our collective shift towards remote working and learning in the wake of the COVID-19 pandemic, there are

thousands of new and innovative ways to learn from experts and facilitators (like me!), explore new skills, and develop existing ones online. Giving your people the freedom to seek out their personal development opportunities might introduce you to new and valuable eLearning platforms (like LinkedIn and Coursera), free resources online (like YouTube video series from experts), and communities that can help your teams thrive (like local or virtual industry-specific meetups).

- **Automation and Streamlining Workflows**
  You know what they say about the phrase "We've always done it that way." It's dangerous in that it prevents innovation and hinders creativity. But what could we achieve if we were willing to help our people automate certain tasks or streamline their workflows through the power of technology? Are there areas within your work that can be addressed through modern solutions to free up time for your teams so they can focus on something that requires more brain power? Things like workflow software, project management tools (like *Monday.com*), Microsoft Suite, and even AI can help your people cut down on busy work and reach for more.

At the end of the day, it's important to remember that it's more than okay to rely on modern tools and technology to help us on our journey to leading thriving teams. If we don't take advantage of the tools at our disposal, we're doing ourselves, our people, and our industries a disservice by closing the door on opportunities for innovation and growth. By stepping out of your comfort zone to try new things and dabble in the digital age, we're better able to keep up with trends, prioritize connectivity, and maximize efficiency in the modern world.

• •

Questions to reflect upon individually, with your team, or let's connect:

1. Do you embrace or resist new technology? What makes you embrace or resist?

2. What new technology have you adopted lately to assist you in being more effective in your work? If you have not adopted anything new lately, what are some areas of technology you could look into to make a difference in your work?

3. Is there a need to review all current technologies being utilized and streamline your current technologies for more clarity in your operating systems?

4. How do you ensure that the integration of new technologies is user-friendly and does not create unnecessary complexity for employees?

5. In what ways do you encourage employees to provide feedback on the usability and effectiveness of the technologies they use, and how does this feedback inform future decisions?

10.

INCENTIVIZING EXCELLENCE
AND CELEBRATING SUCCESS

*"As an effective leader you cannot be concerned
with your individual accomplishments. Your efforts must
be put into building the team and its successes."*
—Stuart Schleien, Professor Emeritus, UNC Greensboro

Motivating your teams toward growth and success is one of the most common topics and questions I encounter when working with leaders across the country. It seems that everybody wants to know some of the most effective ways to inspire growth in their people, and it lights me up to witness such a passion for motivation and celebration of success. The truth is, everyone responds differently to incentivization and rewards, and what works for one person, team, or organization may not work for the next.

Instead of searching for the method of motivation with the highest success rate, I usually recommend that leaders start by observing and interacting intentionally with their teams to figure out what specifically motivates them. There are a few ways to do this, one of which is simply asking your people! That being said, sometimes pay increases or extra PTO (common responses to this question) aren't an option for your organization, and instead of saying "no" in the face of these requests, it might be more beneficial to come up with incentives through careful consideration. A few questions to ask yourself when trying to figure out what might be most effective for your team include:

- What kinds of motivation have worked - or not worked - in the past?

- Do they frequently check in to share their successes and breakthroughs? If so, they may be seeking recognition from you as their leader. Creating a recognition system to share these wins could be a great option!

- Do your teams often spend time together outside of work or schedule happy hours, social outings, or collaborative activities? If so, they might appreciate being recognized in this way!

- Is there a reward or incentive that compliments the task or success?

- Do your people have an opportunity to share their "favorites" during onboarding or check-ins? For example, some leaders introduce a quiz to help determine what their people enjoy doing on the weekends, their favorite sweet treats, which coffee shop they can't live without, etc. This simplifies the process of providing small rewards since you'll always have something to look to for answers.

But before you jump straight into discovering new and effective ways to reward your teams, it's important to clearly define and communicate your expectations so they know what is more likely to result in rewards and incentives. By outlining clear and measurable goals, you can drive your teams to work towards concrete checkpoints and drum up some friendly competition along the way. At the same time, sometimes "just because" recognition is equally as powerful as outlined incentives. When people go above and beyond, bounce back after failure, or bring new ideas to the playing field, we can reward these milestones and inspire others towards these same routes in the process.

There are a few traditional styles of recognition that are tried and true, and I've found that by putting a modern spin on them, we can continue relying on these long-standing methods of incentivization to motivate our teams to greatness.

- **Personal Development Opportunities**
  Some teams are highly motivated by the opportunity to travel to a conference, take an online course, or attend a local networking event to learn more about their interests or develop new skills. If available, encourage team members to inquire about scholarships to attend conferences, especially if your budget is limited. Oftentimes scholarship funding goes unused because people simply do not apply.

- **Public Appreciation and Celebration**
  Camaraderie grows when teams have the chance to recognize and celebrate each other. Implementing employee-of-the-month-style rewards systems can drum up some friendly competition and provide your people with a sense of pride for their work. Additionally, it gives them some positive news to bring home and share with loved ones.

- **Personalized Rewards**
  I mentioned this a little bit already, but by getting to know the likes and preferences of your people, you can simplify the process of providing them with small rewards (like gift cards for coffee, a hand-selected snack for that all-staff meeting, or an anniversary

treat). Instead of assuming everyone wants the same thing, going the extra mile to choose something more personal ensures they feel seen and valued.

> "A lot of my staff are off-site after hours, so there's a little bit of a barrier because we're not sitting in an office together all day. One of the things I do to get to know them is to have them fill out a survey and ask them questions about their favorite candy, drink, etc. Then I will surprise them when they come to their shift on a Saturday morning and their favorite drink is waiting in the fridge for them. It seems so little, but the feedback on those moments is just so great. I think it goes a long way, and those things add up to building a sense of belonging." –Amanda Gehres, Recreation Superintendent, Reynoldsburg Parks & Recreation

- **Team Celebrations and Events**
  This was also mentioned earlier, but for some teams, the collective celebration can be a great way to boost morale, connect outside of the office, and enjoy each other's company in a more personal setting. Rewards like end-of-year parties or quarterly happy hours can help your people develop their relationships and inspire them to continue collaborating. Consider working with stakeholders or partners in the community to host blended events that facilitate more networking.

Remember that effective rewards and recognition should be tailored to serve the needs and preferences of your people, all while aligning with your organizational culture. Some of these options may not work for your teams, but it's important to find something that does. Celebrating the individual and collective successes of your teams recognizes them as humans, deserving of rewards for their hard work and worthy of recognition for the work that they show up to do each day. By caring for our people, we're doing our part as leaders to nurture our most valuable resource.

• •

Questions to reflect upon individually, with your team, or let's connect:

1. How do your team members respond to your current recognition strategies? Is it time to ask them for their insights?

2. What are your current recognition strategies and do you have them associated with goals, strategic plans, or relate them back to your organization's purpose when they are presented?

3. How do you ensure that recognition is timely and consistent, rather than limited to annual performance reviews or specific occasions?

4. Can you share experiences where recognition and incentives positively impacted employee engagement, morale, or overall team performance?

5. How do you ensure that employees at all levels and departments have equal access to recognition and incentives, regardless of their role or function?

11.

GOOD LEADERS
CREATE GREAT LEADERS

*"Leaders need to guide others to uncover
the answer, not tell them the answer."*
−Amy Dingle, Director of Outdoor
Connections, Five Rivers MetroParks

Whether or not you feel totally confident in your ability to lead, you're likely still inspiring the next generation of leaders through your actions and words. Whether it happens by accident or intentionally, nurturing great leaders is an honor that we shouldn't take for granted.

When we're placed into a leadership position or step into the role of a leader, people naturally look to us to set an example, share our wisdom or guidance, and nurture the gifts and talents of others. Some of these people will even find themselves inspired to strive for leadership positions in their own career journeys. Through the process of inspiring this growth across our teams, we're able to compound the knowledge of previous leaders with our own, passing it on to future leaders to create even more effective and refined leadership styles over time.

To put it simply, the biggest takeaways from the leaders before you combined with your own most effective tips will ultimately merge with future leaders' talents and knowledge, too. As we continue to identify and pass along our most incredible tips, insights, and advice to future leaders, we're improving upon the very essence of leadership.

By investing in the growth and development of our people, we're able to strengthen our organization while also cultivating the future leaders who will follow in our footsteps. After traveling around the country and meeting thousands of incredible current and future leaders, I've been able to pick up on a few key strategies for nurturing leadership skills and abilities in others and inspiring them to reach for leadership positions themselves.

- **Encourage self-awareness.**
  We can become the best versions of ourselves (i.e. even better leaders) through the process of reflection, self-awareness, and personal development. If your goal is to help nurture future leaders, you may want to start by instilling habits that help them reflect on their strengths, weaknesses, and values. Through this process, individuals can continually refine their approach to projects, collaboration, and leadership to maximize their impact.

- **Encourage self-leadership.**
  Push past the concept of self-awareness to help educate your people on the power of self-leadership. You can empower your team members to take ownership of their own development wherever possible. Setting personal goals, seeking feedback, and actively pursuing growth opportunities are great ways for individuals to lead themselves toward their fullest potential. By helping them foster this sense of autonomy and accountability, they're able to gain a better understanding of how leadership works.

- **Delegate to support challenging environments.**

  I know I have mentioned delegation before, but it's also one of my most popular conference topic sessions, so I am going to keep reminding you. Take advantage of your opportunity to introduce your potential leaders to different roles, responsibilities, and cross-functional experience. Exposing them to new tasks and opportunities, you're helping them broaden their skills and develop a talent for navigating change (and you just might free yourself up to broaden your own skills - remember you are always developing too). Thriving in new environments will also give them the confidence they need to step up to challenges daily. Next time you're faced with a project or obstacle, ask yourself if you can get your people involved so you can all grow together.

- **Connect through coaching and mentorship.**

  Taking the time to connect one-on-one with your people through regular check-ins, hands-on guidance, and constructive feedback will allow you to encourage and coach potential leaders. Not only will this allow them to get acquainted with your leadership style, but it will also ensure they feel invested in and encouraged on their path to becoming great leaders themselves. You can use this time to catch up, answer their questions, chat through goals, or get involved in their personal development journey. Many organizations develop mentoring programs or offer coaching as an intentional strategy to develop their team members.

- **Introduce leadership development projects or programs.**

  Have you ever thought about creating and introducing your framework for stepping into leadership? Depending on your role and what's already in place at your organization, you might have the opportunity to institute a new way of approaching leadership development. This might look like optional monthly meetings featuring leadership training for those who are interested, or hosting lunch-and-learns to allow your people to learn from outside perspectives. Perhaps you compile your leadership process into a handbook or guide for others to work through independently, and you institute office hours for people to ask questions. Guiding your team through the process of exploring what it means to be a leader can help them take confident steps toward these goals.

It's important to keep in mind that leadership skills are incredibly valuable, even if your organization doesn't currently have opportunities for advancement available, or if your team isn't hiring for leadership positions. Developing leaders benefits everybody, allowing motivated individuals to move forward on their own journey toward success while contributing to the success of others.

· ·

Questions to reflect upon individually, with your team, or let's connect:

1. What are current intentional strategies your organization has to develop leaders?

2. What are the benefits to the individual, team, organization or stakeholders when leadership development is being successfully implemented at an organization?

3. Can you share examples of successful professional development initiatives or programs that have had a positive impact on employee performance and job satisfaction?

4. What steps do you take to assess the current skill sets and learning needs of your employees, and how do you use this information to tailor professional development opportunities?

5. In what ways do you promote cross-functional training and development to foster a more versatile and adaptable workforce?

6. How do you encourage employees to take ownership of their professional development, and what resources or support mechanisms are in place to facilitate self-directed learning?

12.

PRIORITIZING
CHANGE MANAGEMENT

"A sense of resilience is important because our profession is so fluid, constantly changing."
–K D Howell-EL, Recreation Center Director

As much as I wish good intentions were enough to make an impact, none of what I've included in this book so far is relevant if your approach to change management isn't effective. While it's one thing to want better for your team, it's another to put your plan into action, and through the power of change management, anyone can lead their team to greatness. Let's make sure your approach to managing teams through change is both effective and intentional.

Change management is the process of leveraging a structure to transition your teams or individuals from a current state to a desired future state (aka making growth magic happen for your team). By implementing and managing changes in processes, systems, or behaviors, we can achieve our organizational goals. But effective change management requires leaders to both facilitate change and nurture the necessary skills to do so in their employees.

I believe that by adopting a human-centric, empathetic approach, we can effectively drive change within our organizations.

An article from the Center for Creative Leadership[7] notes that "Since change is multifaceted, complex, and continuous, what might seem to be a single change is often anything but — it is a complex change that competes for time, attention, and resources with other changes that are already underway, and those changes yet to be conceived."

For this reason, my own approach to change management has been adapted over time. After several thousands of hours spent working with teams, I've been able to test popular methods (like Harvard Business School's 'power of vision' approach) and adjust them to suit specific teams and individuals. There are a few pieces of the puzzle that I've come to see as non-negotiables, mostly because they always seem to be an effective way to take steps toward growth for teams facing transitions and changes.

1. **Communicate the reason that change is needed.**
    It might sound like a fairly basic reminder, but you might be surprised by how easy it can be to forget to share the "why" with your people. Make sure to outline the need for change and clearly articulate the benefits, long-term vision, and reasoning from the outset. Continuing to repeat and reinforce this "why" can be a great way to keep everyone involved and invested throughout a transition.

2. **Build awareness and create transparency.**
    It can be easy for the importance of change to get lost in the shuffle of driving productivity and transformation at work. Similar to reinforcing the organization-or team-specific "why" behind the change, it can be equally beneficial to remind your people about the benefits of exploring new skills, trying new things,

strengthening resilience, and developing our talents. Creating an open, aware, and transparent environment can create a healthy sense of investment from your people in the change you seek.

3. **Prioritize support and empowerment.**

   When teams lack these elements, change often takes longer than desired. But for leaders who can rally their people each morning, show up with a supportive attitude, and put empowerment at the center of meetings, chats, and check-ins, teams see an impressively smooth transformation. Recognize and reward those who seek and reach for growth, encourage those who struggle, and empower your people through feedback and celebration.

4. **Develop emotional intelligence over time.**

   As we change the way we do things, we must also adjust our mindset towards how we do it - otherwise, we'll revert to our old ways as soon as the timeline is over. If you strive to enhance your emotional intelligence while also encouraging others to do the same, you can all begin to manage emotions and expectations better throughout the process of growing and changing. Navigating change with empathy, compassion, and effective communication can help the process run much more smoothly.

5. **Celebrate creativity and curiosity.**

   I mentioned this a lot in Chapter 7, and I truly believe that this is a huge component of driving effective change among teams. By celebrating the creativity of your people and rewarding curiosity, you can infuse the process of growth and transformation with more enjoyment, more freedom, and more lightheartedness. By keeping the process lighter and brighter, you can prioritize comfort and optimism along the way.

6. **Prepare for resistance and reluctance.**

   We can't expect everyone to be ready, willing, and enthusiastic about every change that comes their way, but we can prepare ourselves for some inevitable friction or hesitancy from our people. Doing so can help protect our egos and give us the foresight to meet resistance with kindness and compassion.

Now, these 6 considerations certainly aren't the *only* way to approach change management, but I've found them to be some of the most impactful ways to show up consistently for teams over time. At the same time, it's important to recognize that change can be difficult. We've all experienced times of change that leave us feeling frustrated, isolated, unsure, or anxious, and it's important to keep that in mind when driving change within your own teams.

Prioritizing patience throughout the process and acknowledging where there's room to slow down can be a great way to create buffer space for potential hang ups without necessarily planning for failure. If you and your team can afford to slow down should things get difficult, I believe that it's important to do so to avoid burnout and anxiety.

. . . .

Questions to reflect upon individually, with your team, or let's connect:

1. What are some strategies you currently have when you are presenting change to those you lead?

2. What are some strategies to improve the way you present change to those you lead?

3. How have you seen people respond to change? What have you learned from their responses that you can instill into your leadership?

4. How do you handle resistance to change, and what steps do you take to address concerns or skepticism among team members or stakeholders?

5. In what ways do you involve and empower team members in the change process, and how does their participation contribute to the success of the initiative?

6. In what ways do you celebrate milestones and successes during the change process, and how does recognition contribute to team morale and motivation?

PART THREE:
DESIGNING

Being intentional is something I'm not willing to compromise on - it allows me to lead teams successfully and in a way that feels comfortable for everyone involved (and if you ask me, avoiding discomfort is non-negotiable).

To me, 'designing' as a leader means being thoughtful, considerate, and intentional in what we do. It means that instead of thoughtlessly implementing, we take time to look at the big picture, consider our decisions' impact on others, and carefully choose what happens next. We take the thoughts, feelings, and capabilities of our team into consideration before delegating, providing feedback, or implementing new processes.

Designing requires us to step back and start by carefully considering the people we're working with and the environment surrounding us. By inviting others into your design process, you will ultimately find more success. It's our job as leaders to make decisions, but that doesn't mean we need to make them alone.

At some point, most leaders realize they hold quite a bit of power over people's experience at work - a place where they spend a significant amount of their lives. Agreeing to be a leader means understanding the weight of this responsibility, and doing everything you can to use it to contribute positively to people's well-being. I believe that it's our job to know our people and their processes intimately and that through close connections and a better understanding of our teams, we can make intentional choices that drive progress.

If our collective goal is to foster a better sense of belonging, the path to get there will almost certainly be paved with intentionality and consideration. Not your strong suit? This section of the book will help you practice these skills to make decisions backed by a conscious effort to put your people first. By intentionally designing processes, structures, and a foundation for your team to grow, you can drive change that feels collaborative, comfortable, and human-centric across your organization.

13.

THE IMPORTANCE OF CREATING AND IMPLEMENTING A SHARED VISION

"Unless the vision is revisited often,
it just becomes words on a page."

–Judd Walker, Director of Student Leadership, Ohio University

The reality of leadership is that obstacles and challenges will inevitably present themselves along your path (sorry, I don't make the rules). But harnessing a future-focused leadership style is one of the best ways you can navigate and overcome these surprises time and time again. Just because they're inevitable doesn't mean they have to be scary.

More than a decade ago, Harvard Business Review conducted a study in which they asked participants about the qualities they desired in colleagues and leaders[8], and the responses still prove relevant today. The most common response was honesty, but the second-highest priority was that a leader be forward-looking, with 72% of respondents noting this as a preference.

In most organizations, non-leadership roles require significantly less focus on the future than leadership roles, which means that for many first-time leaders, this isn't always a skill that comes naturally and might not be an obvious area of focus. For those who are able to harness a forward-focused mindset, however, they can use this skill set to create and share a future-minded vision with others and design stronger, healthier teams.

One particularly relevant Gallup piece[9] states, "There are practical, tangible, measurable ways leaders can properly manage their culture. And it all starts with alignment. Executives need to be on the same page with their leadership teams…about where their culture stands today and where it's headed in the future. You might be thinking: "We're already aligned about our culture." But it's not enough to be generally on the same page. The best leaders are synchronized on specific, seemingly small details about their culture and how they affect performance."

Seasoned leaders tend to agree with this counterintuitive sentiment: focusing on your current state is sometimes the best way to create a vision for your future state. Asking questions about what's currently working - and not working - can help you identify necessary changes and priorities for the future.

Next, you can work together to identify or revise your purpose, mission, and values that will serve as the foundation of your vision. Collaborating to agree on these components is a great way to ensure that everyone feels invested in the vision and ready to work towards it. Your mission and vision statements aren't just meant to serve as sparkly additions to your website or office wallpaper, they should serve as guiding principles for all employees and emanate across meetings and projects, too.

Finally, you can create a strategic plan and identify milestones to help keep you and your team on track and focused on your shared vision. As your team progresses through these milestones, you can reconvene to extend the life of your vision and create new measurable targets to strive for. When it comes to a vision, milestones are less about project success or revenue-specific metrics, and more about culture-related checkpoints, employee and customer satisfaction, and your reputation in the industry.

As you implement this vision, remember that it often takes time for people to reprogram their approach to work and their expectations of the future to align with a new vision. You can reinforce your future-focused mindset through repetition in meetings, and emails, or investing in full-day workshops or facilitators to help keep your team on track. Checking in with your people can be a great way to address pain points and highlights throughout the process, too.

If the idea of creating and implementing a shared vision feels daunting, it might help to think about the benefits and outcomes of doing so. I asked several of my favorite people about how a shared vision contributed to the success of their own teams, here's what they had to say:

1. "We ask ourselves what we are good at and not good at. Is the city ready for this change? Are our partners ready to share our vision with us? As a leader, I need to balance what we are capable of and also new ideas that come from the team. However, as the leader you need to be realistic about what can be accomplished, and you may have to scale down some of their ideas." –Johan Moerman, Board Member & Advisor in the Festival and Cultural Industries, Former CEO of Rotterdam Festivals

2. "People are at their best when they are connected to the purpose of the organization. By having a vision - and a strategic plan to reach that vision - people understand that everyone has a purpose that's tied to that vision. It is also important that people feel like they've got ownership of the vision, and can map it back to their purpose.

We want people to understand their "why". By having the vision and communicating it, you've got something that's providing a framework for decision-making and helps you ask: how does this decision advance us toward our vision? I think it gives team members ownership and creates some accountability, too. Everyone knows they're working for a singular purpose. It makes collaboration easier." –Chad Snow, Chief Operating Officer, BerryDunn

3. "When you have a vision and a sense of purpose, you are not easily distracted. This clarity helps you be an effective worker as well as a strong leader that people want to work with. People want to work for leaders who are also working hard and committed to the same goals. Team members wish to help move the team and unit ahead." –Stuart Schleien, Professor Emeritus, UNC Greensboro

If results like these aren't convincing, just think about the incredible sense of alignment you'll feel across your teams once you find your groove on the path toward embodying your shared vision. Remember that flexing these future-focused muscles takes practice, and creating a vision can't happen overnight. Take your time, practice patience, and enjoy the journey of designing a more aligned culture.

• •

Questions to reflect upon individually, with your team, or let's connect:

1. How do you define the concept of a "shared vision" in the context of leadership, and why do you consider it important for a successful workplace?

2. Can you share an example from your leadership experience where a shared vision played a pivotal role in achieving a significant team or organizational goal?

3. What are intentional strategies you have to keep your team/organization focused on a shared vision?

4. What are challenges to keeping a shared vision throughout all levels of the organization? What are ideas to overcome these challenges?

5. In what ways do you use visual representations, such as vision boards, pocket cards, or visual storytelling, to reinforce and internalize the shared vision among team members?

14.

BACK TO THE BASICS: UNDERSTANDING YOUR "WHO"

"Everyone needs to feel they are part of the team and their opinions, concerns, and ideas are welcome."
–Mark Mostar, RN

'm going to suggest an exercise that most people think they don't need. Stay with me here, because there's a reason I've chosen to talk about this in this section of the book. It's essential, so even if your initial reaction is to assume you don't need it or that you've done it recently enough to disregard the suggestion, I highly encourage you to consider paying this chapter special attention.

Despite frequent contact, close proximity, or even solidified work friendships, it can be easy to forget to really, truly, deeply consider the people you work with. You might even know their kids' names, where they like to travel during holiday weekends, or that they have therapy appointments every other Wednesday, but a work environment has a funny way of making us feel like we're more in tune with each other than we really are.

As leaders, I think we owe it to our people to take time out of our busy schedules to seriously think about their needs, wants, abilities, concerns, circumstances, and interests. By prioritizing an intimate understanding of who we work with, we can ensure that our decisions are made with them in mind. It's the difference between knowing their favorite vacation destination and having a deep understanding of what matters to them at work. This intentional approach to leadership is what allows us to create structure, build a foundation, and design services that are effective and impactful.

Since it can be so easy to dismiss exercises that help you understand your people, I'm sharing three of my favorite ways you can practice mindfulness when it comes to your teams:

1. **Ask more personal questions during check-ins.** For example, maybe you have weekly standing meetings with each of your people and can choose one specific question to ask everyone, focusing on specific topics where work and life intersect. My Team Talk Cards (mentioned in Chapter 2) simplify this step exponentially; here are some additional ideas:

   ○ What are you looking forward to in and outside of work this month?

   ○ If our team could volunteer for a day, where would you suggest we volunteer?

   ○ Who is one person you would like to have lunch with at this organization and why?

   ○ Have you learned a new skill (personal or professional) in the past three months?

   ○ What are you watching or reading right now, and do you have recommendations to share?

- Which of your teammates would you like to recognize and why?

- How do you think we could improve the culture and morale of our team?

2. **Instead of assuming, get them involved.** When the opportunity arises to delegate projects, decide on professional development opportunities, or plan the next team meeting, invite your people to join in on the conversation. Not only will this allow you to field their thoughts and requests, but you might also learn a little bit about what's important to each of them along the way. Where do their passions and interests lie, and how can you use those to your advantage - and theirs? Or better yet, have them schedule the next professional development training or create a cross-division professional development committee to plan training needs and create a schedule of available opportunities.

3. **Take advantage of opportunities to connect.** This might seem obvious, but ask yourself how many times your people have extended an olive branch and you haven't reached out to grab it. When employees share details about their lives with you (like what they're watching or reading, where they like to eat, their latest work-mode playlist, or something useful in their workspace), we have the opportunity to accept and indulge these bids for connection. Watching that TV show, listening to that playlist, or ordering that $5 organizer for their desk drawer might make all the difference in getting to know them better, giving you something to connect about, and deepening your relationships across the team. The next time someone lets you in on a slice of their life, ask yourself how you can engage with it in a meaningful way.

Exercises that help you consider your people and prioritize their perspectives can have an instantaneous impact on the quality of collaboration and connection across your teams. Truthfully, it isn't enough to just know your people, you have to put them first whenever possible, too.

When I asked my network to share some of their favorite ways to keep their people top of mind, here's what they shared:

1. "I really make a point to chat with my people. When I took this new position, I scheduled one-on-one meetings with every person on my team. And I remind them that I care about them as a human more than I care about them as a professional. If they have a family, I don't want them missing the kids' games. I want them to come and talk to me, because I know that your family should be the most important thing to you, too." –Manny Padia, Recreation Administrator

2. "At our monthly meetings, we start off with a temperature check. We will ask, "From 1 to 10, what is your temperature reading today, personally or professionally, and why?" We come into the space with an open mind that not everyone feels like a 10 and we allow folks to be a 2 or 3, and it could be something work-related or not work-related that is giving them their temperature reading. However, I want to know what [they] are dealing with and know that not everything has to be about work and work only. Yes, it is work, but it's also that person. There is a personal side to everyone that we should get to know too, because we may be going through the same thing." –Steven Carter, Deputy Director, Maryland-National Park/Planning Commission

3. "To ensure I'm being considerate of others, I ask them how they feel respected. When I'm bringing together a new team, I'll ask

this question of everyone in the group, and we'll share our answers publicly. This ensures we're all on the same page as we develop norms within our team." –Judd Walker, Director of Student Leadership, Ohio University

4. "I try to have lunch with my team and peers on a monthly basis at a minimum. This casual offsite approach allows for us to decompress and effectively communicate without the phone calls, emails, and day-to-day tasks bogging us down." –Jennifer Kempert, Recreation & Special Events Coordinator

5. "I walk by every person's office almost daily, even if it's for a simple, "Hello, how's your day going? How was your weekend? Do you have any big plans?" Questions non-related to work help build rapport and learn more about those we work alongside. Building rapport helps build loyalty, and as a leader, we cannot just expect loyalty, rather we need to build relationships within the organization through intentional actions of our own." –Kevin Grothe, Vice President of Sponsorships, Memphis in May International Festival

These are just a few of the accessible, simple ways I like to suggest leaders get to know their people better, but don't forget that opportunities for connection present themselves every day. What might happen if you reached out to say good morning more often, or spent a few more minutes chatting about the weekend on Mondays? Nurturing these connections is a great first step toward being an unwaveringly intentional leader.

• •

Questions to reflect upon individually, with your team, or let's connect:

1. What are three intentional strategies *(I challenge you to try some new strategies if you're already good and connecting with your team)* you will implement this week to learn or learn more about your 'who'?

2. Do you know your team members professional journey and what led them to their current role?

3. Do you know what your team members love most about their job and/or which tasks or projects they find most fulfilling?

4. How do people in your organization/your team handle stress or tight deadlines, and is there anything specific they find helpful in managing workload pressures?

5. What is one thing you'd like others to know about your preferred work environment or conditions that help you perform at your best?

15.

HOW TO BE A SOCIAL ENGINEER

"A true, next level, evolutionary leader, is a person who can respond to others egos and skill sets and ultimately equalize the room, the conversation, and space."
–Lisa Paradis, Consultant, BerryDunn

What's a social engineer? To put it simply, a social engineer is anyone who manages social change. As leaders, we all have an opportunity to serve as social engineers within our organization and can manage social change over time. By leveraging the talents, interests, and perspectives of our people, we can drive progress, productivity, connection, and engagement across teams. This act of designing an intentional workplace and nurturing collaboration across individuals and teams is one of the best ways to drive efficient change. When people are willing and eager to work together and feel confident and comfortable in their roles, big things happen (sometimes even with a smile).

Expecting a group (of any size) to automatically get along, work well together, and know how to collaborate efficiently isn't reasonable. Not only does it take time for people to get to know each other well enough to function efficiently, but it also requires quite a bit of work on your part as a leader and guide throughout the process. Designing and engineering change, growth, and collaboration within your people should - of course - be done with intention. A few ways I like to strategically encourage collaboration and supportively engineer connection include:

- Placing two team members together for a project to improve collaboration

- Create cross-division teams to work on strategic goals

- Encourage team members to get involved with task force groups outside of their own divisions, departments, or resource groups

- Invite other departments to join in on meetings

When reaching out to my community of friends and fellow leaders, they also shared some priceless wisdom about how they approach social engineering through an intentional lens within their teams. Here's what they had to say:

1. "During meetings, I have team members share about their areas to develop an appreciation and understanding of what other areas are doing. Everyone thinks their job is harder than others, or that others have it easier – we try to break down this thinking. We are all serving the community through the work we do. We try to build compassion and understanding for one another's work." –Erica Perez, Recreation Manager

2. "I give people roles and responsibilities that are vital to the success of the change and growth, and I acknowledge individual accomplishments as we collectively work towards that change. This requires a deft touch to ensure work is equitable. Folks should not feel consistently overwhelmed or bored. People will do the work

if they feel like they are contributing to something meaningful."
–Judd Walker, Director of Student Leadership, Ohio University

3. "As leaders we have the ability to intentionally look at how we engineer our people towards their own individual growth along with organizational growth. We must know the strengths of our team members in order to socially engineer and lead effectively. I spend the first hour of my day alone in my office (door closed) to thoughtfully prepare my day and organize my own thoughts to strategically think about how I will best mobilize my team. I need to think through what the plays of the day may be and remove obstacles and barriers for my team. This intentional time each morning also provides me with time to engineer my own reactions and monitor any potential barriers I could bring to situations."
    –Patrick Hammer, Director of Parks and Recreation, Town of Erie

These examples and insights highlight the importance of fostering open communication, focusing on individuals' strengths, and encouraging frequent collaboration. But why is it so important to sharpen our social engineering skills? Not only does this skill set allow us to nurture connection and productivity in our current state, but part of being a social engineer is also about keeping an eye on the future and preparing to navigate big changes down the road.

As you identify long-term goals for your team and your organization, it's important to identify milestones that will help get you there. Social engineering with intention is what allows us to harness foresight to instill the qualities we know we'll need to overcome obstacles that we've identified in these future-focused plans, building resilience in our people to navigate challenges gracefully.

In addition to the powerful sentiments noted above, I also believe it's crucial to understand individual strengths, provide development opportunities, lead by example, promote work-life balance, and provide feedback and growth opportunities.

Building a positive, inclusive, engaged work culture ultimately benefits everyone involved. Not only do individuals find more meaning and connection within their roles, but productivity and engagement skyrocket as we develop, design, and engineer social environments with intention.

• •

Questions to reflect upon individually, with your team, or let's connect:

1. How do you approach social engineering (the act of guiding growth and change among people) through an intentional lens within your own teams?

2. What do you do to social engineer collaboration with grace and care?

3. Can you share examples of initiatives you've implemented to improve team communication and strengthen relationships among team members?

4. Can you share experiences where you've successfully integrated new team members into the existing social fabric of the team?

5. What steps do you take to ensure that the positive social dynamics cultivated within the team extend to interactions with other departments or external stakeholders?

16.

INNOVATING WITH INTENTION

"When you're being innovative, you have to be willing to put yourself at risk of not knowing the outcome."
—Bernita, Director

A few chapters back, I shared some of my insights on the importance of creating and implementing a shared vision. A high-powered vision put into action is one of the best ways to create a foundation for your team that inspires innovation and enables you to design a forward-thinking workforce with intention. So, if a high-powered and innovative team is on your vision board, you're already on the right track.

Innovation is one of those buzzwords (yeah, I said it) that is consistently injected into conversations, usually in an effort to convey a sense of creative or futuristic thinking or a desire to set a tone in the industry. And while it's great to aspire to be ahead of the curve and on the cusp of trending technology or practices, let's reel it back in to focus on what innovation truly means (because, surprise, it's more than just trendsetting).

When it comes to leadership and leading teams within an organization, innovation takes shape as a *collective* ability and desire to challenge the status quo through inventive thinking, creativity, and a willingness to explore new opportunities.

> "As leaders we need to nurture innovation. I have noticed when our team isn't innovating, we aren't at our best." –Patrick Hammer, Director of Parks and Recreation, Town of Erie

Not only are innovative teams interested in the next big things, but they're doing the work to research, prepare, and implement throughout projects. Additionally, they feel confident in their decisions when branching off or ditching old solutions.

Blockbuster (remember them?) may have been interested in innovating, but in 2000, they collectively decided not to take advantage of the opportunity to purchase Netflix for $50 million. We can learn from this example by ditching arrogance for openness and competition for collaboration.

As a leader, how can you instill a heightened sense of innovation in your people? And how can you ensure that innovation is a piece of the foundation or vision that serves as a source of inspiration for your collective work?

First, I'll share a few of my own tips, and then I'll share a few can't-miss insights from a few of my high-caliber connections in the leadership space:

- **Establish a shared vision**. I know, I know, we've been over this. I can't emphasize enough the importance of incorporating innovation and innovative practices into your shared vision. Through repetition and shared goals, you and your team can work towards harnessing an innovative mindset throughout all that you do, allowing you to focus your innovation toward relevant goals, obstacles, and areas of interest over time. This extra intention placed on your vision can make the difference between chaos and intentional design.

- **Encourage autonomy and provide resources.** If you want to foster more innovation, make sure your people know they don't have to ask for permission to think outside the box or reach outside of the mold. Nurture their sense of independence, especially when it comes to problem-solving, and provide them with resources to help them go the extra mile. Resources might include access to third-party learning platforms (like MasterClass or Skillshare), a fresh environment to collaborate together in person (like a monthly workday from a local library or coffee shop), or access to your network of experts across topics they might be eager to explore.

- **Champion innovation...loudly.** Many of us know the benefits of rewarding behaviors we want to see more of. Incentivizing your people to be innovative is often an impactful way to remind them that out-of-the-box thinking won't end up being scolded or undervalued. It can be stressful to go out on a limb and suggest or try something new, but by rewarding innovation when you see it, your teams will quickly realize that it isn't as scary as it might seem. By incentivizing the specific kinds of innovation you want to see (for example, as it relates to technology, collaborative exercises, structure, or information sharing), you can intentionally design a team of thoughtful forward thinkers.

- **Break down barriers when possible.** Part of your vision might (er, should) be to identify and remove any organizational barriers that disrupt or prevent innovation. Depending on your organization, you might not be able to remove every barrier that exists, but creating space and eliminating friction where possible can create a supportive structure, allowing for agile decision-making and more efficient implementation of fresh ideas. You might need to dissect current processes and procedures, assessing how much freedom team members have to make decisions. Some leaders elect to set aside an "innovation budget," creating more space for people to try new things.

- **Track team progress and prepare to pivot**. By monitoring your team's progress on an innovative front, you can provide ongoing feedback and nurture a sense of openness to adaptation. If you can't adapt, you can't evolve, so this step is key in making sure your team can innovate like a well-oiled machine. Make adjustments to your approach to innovation based on outcomes, insights, and findings along the way. This is a great way to ensure your people feel supported in their efforts, too. I can vouch for a book called The Invisible Advantage[3] from Soren Kaplan, which includes a survey that can help you assess your company culture as it relates to innovation.

Here's how some of my colleagues and connections put these practical tips on display for their own teams:

1. "You have to make time for innovation - if you only stay focused on the practical things you need to do every day, [innovation] won't happen. As a leader, you have to try to create an organization that is welcoming to wild ideas and has time to develop them. Sometimes, when you start something innovative, it looks inefficient or hard to reach – but if people are enthusiastic about the idea, you should try it." –Johan Moerman, Board Member & Advisor in the Festival and Cultural Industries, Former CEO of Rotterdam Festivals

2. "The biggest enemy of any organization is complacency. Just because you did something last year, and you were successful… you [still] need to reinvent yourself. And in order to do that, you

need to innovate. Innovation can be something as small as an internal change that makes getting client work done easier and more efficient. Innovation helps drive growth and it helps keep us competitive. Clients want to know they're going to be working with a firm that is bringing innovative approaches to them. So if you've got a fast-moving business, being accustomed to innovation makes the adaption and adoption of change easier. It helps foster continuous improvement in the organization as well. If you're innovating, it also conditions your employees for change. If you are status quo for 10 years and then you need to implement innovation or change, think about how much more difficult it will be to motivate the people within your organization." –Chad Snow, Chief Operating Officer, BerryDunn

3. "You create a culture where people feel like they can suggest changes or new ideas. You listen when they share those, and guide them in the direction where they can determine if it is a good idea or not. You never shut it down!" –Dianna Lawrence, Superintendent of Community Events, City of Richardson

· ·

Questions to reflect upon individually, with your team, or let's connect:

1. How do you define an innovative mindset, and why do you believe it's important for the success of a team or organization?

2. How do you help promote an innovative mindset across teams and remove barriers that make innovation feel daunting or difficult?

3. Why is an innovative spirit so important to nurture as a leader, and what are some of your favorite outcomes of successfully cultivating innovation within teams or individuals?

4. How do you stay informed about industry trends, emerging technologies, and best practices, and how does this knowledge influence your approach to fostering innovation?

5. How do you balance the need for structured processes with the flexibility required for creative thinking and experimentation?

17.

AVOIDING SILOS WITHIN YOUR ORGANIZATION

"Life is much richer and fulfilling when you're able to accomplish things together as part of a team."
—Stuart Schleien, Professor Emeritus, UNC Greensboro

Sometimes, despite our best intentions, our efforts to encourage collaboration and connection across teams result in tight-knit groups that need help to work with those outside of their immediate unit. And while it's ultimately a good thing that we've nurtured the connection *within* these individual units, an inability to collaborate externally is a sure sign of a siloed organization. Helping your people expand their collaborative abilities beyond their own teams is critical to the success of your mission, your vision, and your organization as a whole. So how can you both avoid silos within your teams and also help existing silos branch out?

My biggest piece of advice is to nurture and facilitate cross-functional teams within your department and organization. Like most things, this is much easier said than done. But the benefits of creating effective and efficient cross-functional teams are irresistible, allowing you to intentionally design a powerful, cohesive team.

When it comes to developing your cross-functional teams, the goal is to form partnerships consisting of individuals in different departments (or areas of specialty). Not only does this encourage the adoption of a broader perspective, but it also allows teams to work on specific projects together, encouraging the spread of diverse insights, experiences, and backgrounds. Many leaders of high-functioning teams cite their emphasis on cross-functionality as their golden ticket to success. I asked a few all-star leaders from my network to share their own perspectives:

1. "To achieve next-level collaboration, we have to be able to embrace the dissenter in a group. We have to embrace the people that say things that might not align with how you are thinking and stay curious about their thoughts in order to collaborate. What they say may be prickly and even uncomfortable, but stay open, as it may elicit good ideas. These dissenters can sometimes feel combative to you but I think when we embrace one another, a team gets that piece of culture right." –Lisa Paradis, Consultant, BerryDunn

2. "Communication is different for each person. Some are no-nonsense and want to get right to the point - others love to talk about family vacations and hobbies. Therefore, you have to get to know your coworkers and adjust your communication methods to what they're receptive to. This is important for creating safe spaces, collaboration and transparent relationships. It brings in a sense of belonging and it speaks to the importance of how small interactions can have big results. Work environments are all cultural, and how you build culture will impact results. You can have all the policies you want in place, but it's the culture that surrounds policies and the environment that you create that gets results.

It's you knowing I have others' best interest in mind, not just my own." –Kevin Grothe, Vice President of Sponsorships, Memphis in May International Festival

3. "Culture trumps strategy, strategy drives structure, structure facilitates outcomes, and outcomes achieve the mission. That is a guiding principle – it's written on my whiteboard, and I reference it a lot because I can compartmentalize different parts of collaboration, culture, and functionality within those 4 areas. I think it's important to always have a pulse on where you are with that." –Amy Dingle, Director of Outdoor Connections, Five Rivers MetroParks

By taking notes from experts like these and identifying relevant tactics that might work for your specific teams and industry, you can effectively tailor your approach to nurturing connectivity. Remember that when working with more than a few people at a time, it takes a lot of trial and error to discover what kinds of activities, encouragement, or tactics work best. Have patience and keep in mind that by being intentional in your actions throughout the process, you'll be well-equipped to leverage effective teamwork to bring your visions to life.

• •

Questions to reflect upon individually, with your team, or let's connect:

1. How do you define effective collaboration?

2. What do you do to help nurture cross-functionality and collaboration among teams or individuals?

3. Why are cross-functional capabilities such an important element of workplace culture, and how do they contribute to an intentionally designed workplace?

4. Can you share experiences where cross-functional collaboration led to successful outcomes, and what lessons were learned from those experiences?

5. How do you balance individual contributions with the collective goals of the team, ensuring that everyone feels valued and heard in the collaborative process?

18.

REFRAMING FAILURE AND EMBRACING RISK

"Without failure, one will never truly appreciate success."
–Kenny Patterson, Sr. Director -
Implementation, Sunland Logistics Solutions

One of the more impactful ways we can design a culture and workplace full of belonging, comfort, and support is by reframing the way we collectively look at failure. Embracing risk is something that most people think either comes easily or not at all, but thankfully, it can be learned (trust me, I did it myself). Why is it so important to help our people develop a better tolerance of risk, and inspire them to reframe their outlook on failure? Because it minimizes the impact that obstacles and challenges have while simultaneously improving morale in the face of setbacks. A double whammy, if you ask me.

The concept of a growth mindset, which I mentioned earlier in sections one and two of this book, is all about reframing the way we look at failure and shifting our perspective to focus on opportunities for growth in the face of a challenge. As a result of harnessing a growth mindset and strengthening your ability to reframe failure, you'll undoubtedly grow better at embracing risk, too, allowing you to design a more comfortable and confident culture. Some of the benefits of this shift include:

- Less anxiety about uncertainty

- Faster bounce-back times following a failure

- Increased confidence, unwavering in the face of challenges

- More effective collaboration despite disruptions

- Heightened morale across teams and organizations

- Redirected focus toward opportunities and new ideas

- Increased sense of empowerment

- Minimized sense of anxiety, frustration, and rejection

- Consistent and steady levels of optimism

...to name a few. But emphasizing or encouraging a perspective shift and actually helping them to nurture one are two totally different tasks. There are a few ways I try to set teams up for success as they work towards this mindset adjustment together.

First, remind your teams that placing blame isn't the priority. Failure, mistakes, challenges, or roadblocks are usually the result of something more than just one person's actions. And even if they *are* the result of one person's actions or choices, it doesn't do anyone any good to point fingers, feel shame, or place blame. I strive to highlight the benefits of skipping the blame-game step, reminding my people that it's not necessary to waste energy or time feeling guilty toward ourselves or frustrated by others for a poor outcome or unexpected failure.

Next, take stock of findings and learning opportunities. You might even find that it's fairly easy to get your team excited about what was learned in the process of stumbling or failing. Working together to create a big list of what you now know thanks to a recent challenge is a great way to put a positive spin on the experience and look on the bright side. During this step, I think it's important to highlight the incredible opportunities that taking risks often brings us. This will help bolster their ability to embrace risky decisions, leading to a greater willingness to get creative and think outside the box.

Finally, and this tends to work best when done consistently over time, it's important to share personal stories of failure and lean into learning moments to destigmatize the concept as a whole. The more we normalize failing, stumbling, and encountering obstacles, the less difficult it becomes to work through these happenings with a level head, confidence, and clarity. As leaders, we have the opportunity to lead by example, which means we can be totally honest about how it feels to fail (let's face it, it sucks) while also exemplifying what it looks like to face challenges head-on and with a positive attitude. Doing so is a great way to teach your people that failure can result in learning opportunities, and shouldn't cause us to shy away from taking risks or exploring new paths. Check out the Love, Low, Learn template at *anniefrisoli.com* to guide you in a conversation with your team.

Reframing failure and embracing risk isn't just a valuable skill in the workplace. As you and your people work towards a more resilient mindset, and your intentional efforts to design a more confident workspace pay off, you and your team might notice the benefits of this growth mindset beyond the confines of work. In general, this shift can lead to a healthier mindset throughout all walks of life, making this an exceptionally valuable skill to invest in.

• •

Questions to reflect upon individually, with your team, or let's connect:

1. How do you balance the need for caution with the importance of taking risks in your professional life?

2. What is your approach to learning from failures without dwelling on them?

3. Can you think of a situation where taking a calculated risk led to positive outcomes?

4. How do you assess and manage risk in your decision-making process?

5. How do you encourage a growth mindset within yourself or your team?

PART FOUR:
BELONGING

L ast, but certainly not least, we've come to what might be my favorite section of this book: belonging. It's my favorite because I believe that if we do enough of the right things (and notice that I didn't say 'if we do everything right,' because that would be impossible), we can leverage the sense of belonging as a catalyst to do almost anything and everything else.

When people feel they belong, they're more likely to contribute, engage, collaborate, take risks, remain authentic, dedicate themselves to their work, and remain committed to their team and organization's mission. Happy, engaged employees contribute more, bring their passion to the table, and inspire others through a positive attitude. And when we surround ourselves with people like this, and ensure that they feel they belong, we accomplish more in less time, we reach new heights, we break the mold, and we create happy, high-performing teams. We succeed.

Not only does company culture play a massive role in overall satisfaction levels at work, but it also contributes to a better, brighter world. Leadership is important within organizations, but our reach extends far beyond what happens in the office. Leading people through change, championing their accomplishments, and ensuring they feel safe and seen at work can actually contribute to the bigger picture. Remember when I said that people are our superpower?

Beyond the workplace, people who are happy in their jobs go out into the world and contribute positively to society. They feel more satisfied, supported, and willing to support others, too. What a beautiful opportunity we have to brighten our own corners of the world through effective leadership and a sense of belonging.

In an effort to inject this world - and your workplace - with more belonging, I put this sentiment at the heart of my mission. Building a sense of belonging and community within your own workplace requires a whole lot of the intentionality I harped on in the previous section. Belonging can be designed through intentional efforts, and now that you've harnessed my insights on how to remain intentional, you'll be able to take big steps toward nurturing a sense of belonging within your own teams.

This section will cover several of my favorite ways to take care of your people and solidify a sense of belonging that opens doors for possibility within your organization. Through community, connection, comfort, and inclusion, I believe we can accomplish anything. As the saying goes…

Alone we can go fast. Together we can go far.

19.

BUILD, MAINTAIN,
OR BREAK DOWN

"Culture ebbs and flows daily."
–Amy Dingle, Director of Outdoor Connections,
Five Rivers MetroParks

E very time you interact with someone, it's an opportunity to build, maintain, or break down that relationship - if you've heard me speak or participated in one of my sessions, you know how strongly I feel about this concept. Whether you're passing by in a hallway, stuck in a pre-meeting waiting room together, or meeting up for your regularly scheduled check-in, you can leverage your interactions to make an impact on your overall relationships.

While it might seem like some interactions are negligible (like sharing a 30-second elevator ride, standing next to each other in the buffet line at a conference, or bumping into each other outside of work), no encounter is too small to serve as an opportunity for intentional growth and development. We can harness these opportunities and use them to design the workplace of our dreams, leveraging them to build, grow, deepen, strengthen, and solidify our relationships.

Unfortunately for me, it took me quite a while to realize the gravity and power of my words and actions, especially when it comes to influencing others and engineering a comfortable, energizing workplace. But now, I get to help you learn from my mistakes, and avoid a too-late realization that you hold the power to influence others for good.

The difference between building and breaking down a relationship is probably fairly clear, but what does it mean to maintain relationships, and is it beneficial? First, let's dissect each of these approaches to relationship management:

Building relationships involves an active pursuit of a deeper, more meaningful connection. It means striving to know someone more intimately and in a way that allows you to remain considerate in leading them or working with them. Building relationships requires more than the occasional check-in or friendly banter and can be achieved through intentional outreach, asking follow-up questions, recognition, consideration, and appreciation. If your conversations or interactions with a colleague start to feel templated, predictable, or casual, you may be merely maintaining.

Maintaining relationships involves the templated, predictable, and casual approach I just mentioned. Sometimes, even though we feel like saying good morning or chatting about the weekend is actively building a relationship, it's merely maintaining one. While this chatter is well-intentioned, it doesn't actively develop your connection or deepen your relationship. Now, if your relationship is in a good place and doesn't require development, this may be a perfectly effective approach for certain connections. But if it feels like something is missing, or like your connection with a colleague would benefit from some extra attention, you'll want to switch out of maintenance mode and into a more intentional investment state of mind.

Breaking down relationships involves underinvesting, withdrawing, actively criticizing, belittling, or neglecting your connections. While sometimes it involves a negative approach, it can also come from a lack of commitment or presence during conversations or time together. When an encounter presents itself, actions that don't reflect a sense of enthusiasm or interest in your people may contribute to a breakdown of your bond. In fact, being unintentional, unaware, or uninvested in *actively* building your relationships can have negative impacts, as your lack of presence and intention may be construed as disinterest. Unless your goal is to burn a bridge or let a relationship fizzle, it's important to avoid this underwhelming approach to relationship management.

If your goal is to be a leader who continually builds others up and nurtures your relationships, however, it might require some intentional shifts in how you approach interactions. As I mentioned earlier, many of us only maintain our relationships without realizing that we aren't growing them. Here are some of my favorite ways to actively and intentionally grow relationships and great a more profound sense of belonging within teams:

- **Go old school with a hand-written note**. For years I have kept thank you cards at my desk to ensure I keep up this important habit. But, for those of you that do not keep stamps handy, an intentional strategy my dear friend, colleague, business coach, and 9-time TEDx speaker Blake Fly[10] taught me was to write a quick note on a piece of paper, snap a photo of it, and then send a picture of that handwritten note in a text. People will appreciate the "handwritten" text message.

- **Video messages vs. written messages**. I am a big fan of sending team members a video greeting. For example, prior to working with teams, I may send them a video while out hiking. I do this to show the human side of me, share my "home" area with them, and provide a sense of connection prior to meeting them.

- **Bring others into the connection**. I asked members of my Facebook community to become Secret Agents of Spreading Kindness. 40 people said YES to the idea, which involved identifying one person a month to collectively make a positive impact on. We all sent pump-up messages to a college basketball coach on his first game of the season. Another mission we all participated in was sending someone condolences after her dad passed. We even sent 40 text messages wishing a very special person a happy 80th birthday. Collective gratitude is an excellent way to build belonging among team members.

- **Send a photo**. If I see something that reminds me of someone in my contact list, I will pause to text them a photo. While on vacation, I saw a guitar player who looked like a grad student of mine from 10 years ago. I snapped a photo of the entertainer and sent it to my former student and asked him if he had changed careers - this prompted a few quick texts to one another and in one of his responses, he said thanks for reaching out and expressed that it was good to connect.

- **Send them a cup of coffee**. I usually title my virtual meetings with people "Coffee Talk: *Their Name* x Annie." Prior to the meeting, I will use *Thnks.com* to send a virtual coupon for a cup of coffee. I will also use this website to recognize people for varying accomplishments, as an act of gratitude, or even once as an apology for missing a meeting.

• •

Questions to reflect upon individually, with your team, or let's connect:

1. In what ways do you foster trust when establishing new connections?

2. What strategies do you use to remember and recall important details about people you meet?

3. How do you navigate building professional relationships in a virtual or remote work environment?

4. Can you share an example of a mentor or role model who has influenced your approach to relationship building?

5. What steps do you take to expand your network and build connections within your industry or community?

6. In what ways do you contribute to creating a positive and inclusive atmosphere within a team or community?

20.

THERE'S UNITY IN VARIETY

"I met people from all walks of life and just because they were different from me, I didn't give it much thought. If they were genuine, I would focus on that."
–Anthony Frisoli, aka Dad

We're all vastly different. From our heads to our toes and every last cell in between, we look, feel, think, act, and evolve differently than anyone else. At the same time, there's a bit of a stigma that surrounds us, especially at work, and it often leads us to believe that our differences are a bad thing, rather than the superpower that they really are. The things that make us different are actually the same things that make us great candidates, teammates, and leaders, and I think it's time we really embrace them.

When it comes to embracing our differences, it's important to consider the perspectives and preconceptions that we bring to the workplace. By breaking down ideas of what people "should" be like, we can begin to embrace the uniqueness that surrounds us. Here are a few perspectives from my network:

1. "Once we started hiring people that didn't look exactly like us, a lot more people started joining the team that also didn't look like

us, and they had a lot of different perspectives to offer. Once we became intentional, our workforce has also become more diverse, again, matching our community. I think that diversity breeds diversity because people feel more comfortable when they see people who look like them at the front desk or at the after-school program or at the sports program." –Miranda Gomez, Community Services Director, City of Buckeye

2. "By bringing in a team of people from various backgrounds and demographics, I have been able to enhance creativity, innovation, and organizational growth. Everyone brings their own unique perspective to the table and when we are able to give a voice to people with life and professional experiences different from our own, we can achieve greater success." –Mairin Petrone, Executive Director, Pittsburgh Irish Festival

At work, there should always be room for unique experiences, skill sets, perspectives, brainstorming styles, and interests. By creating room and a safe space for these differences to shine and add value, we're simultaneously encouraging growth, collaboration, trust, innovation, acceptance, creativity, and curiosity. And, as we've already acknowledged throughout this book, all of those things work together to drive success and empower a sense of belonging at work.

One of the most difficult situations I find myself in when working with a new team is when they have been conditioned to believe that the way it's always been done is the only way to do things. The we've-always-done-it-this-way mold can be dangerous, and if a previous leader or the procedures in place created a workplace where doing things differently wasn't acceptable, growth and satisfaction are usually lacking. Additionally, these teams usually require quite a bit extra patience and nurturing to break through these mental barriers and embrace their diverse ways of thinking, acting, feeling, and existing.

To help teams unlearn this rigid approach and instead, embrace their diversity, I leverage a lot of the tools and approaches mentioned in chapters 7, 10, and 18. Encouraging curiosity, rewarding results that challenge the status quo, and reframing failure can help teams gain a better understanding of the importance of diversity and unique approaches. But beyond these examples, there are a few ways I like to help other leaders embrace and encourage diversity within their teams.

- **Get comfortable with the fact that leadership isn't one-size-fits-all**. You won't be able to lead all of your people in the same way, and you'll have to meet them where they are if you hope to drive effective and efficient work. Acknowledging this is a great first step in actually adjusting your leadership styles based on the diverse needs and interests of your team members. This barrier is usually bigger than we realize, and if we can break it down within our own thought processes, we can show up in a way that authentically embraces differences.

- **Give everyone a chance to lead**. Doing so can actually nudge people out of their comfort zone far enough to realize that challenging the status quo is expected and embraced. Whether you give everyone the chance to present their expertise, share a project, or spotlight something totally unrelated to work, this can put diversity on display and give your people a chance to recognize and appreciate their differences.

- **Prioritize connection before content**. If your team is struggling to accept, embrace, or harness their diverse backgrounds, spend some time at your next meeting going through exercises that allow your people to learn more about the diverse backgrounds they bring to their roles, and help them understand how these qualities contribute to a richer, more inspiring environment at work. These exercises can help people feel appreciated, and remind them to bring their authentic selves to their jobs - and to remind us that at the center of every employee is a human.

- **Continue hiring diverse talent.** Next time you're hiring, remember that with each hire you have the opportunity to bring fresh eyes, fresh perspectives, and fresh talent to your team. Instead of seeking out the perfect fit or a personality match that might blend in, embrace the wonderfully diverse backgrounds that present themselves, and ask yourselves how their unique perspective might be able to energize your existing team.

  > During my career as a lecturer I taught at a university where I was the only female faculty member in the Recreation Studies program. After teaching at this university for a couple of years, a female student approached me to express the impact my teaching had on her. She chose to declare recreation as a major after finally seeing someone that looked like her represented in the field.

Through consistent encouragement, acknowledgment, celebration, and leading by example, we can help teams shake the status quo and embrace the diversity within all of us. In doing so, we foster more inclusive, accepting workspaces and contribute to an unshakable sense of belonging within our workplace.

• •

Questions to reflect upon individually, with your team, or let's connect:

1. How do you define diversity within the context of a work team, and why is it important to you?

2. How do you promote an inclusive culture that values and respects the unique contributions of each team member?

3. What steps do you take to ensure that diverse voices are heard and valued during team meetings and decision-making processes?

4. How do you ensure that diversity is not just a checkbox but a fundamental aspect of the team's identity and culture?

21.

CREATING BELONGING FROM THE START

*"No matter your title or position you
must respect and appreciate all colleagues.
If people are respected and appreciated,
they tend to want to become better in any situation."*
—Chris Perko, aka Annie's Favorite Sister

S o far, I've covered several solutions and approaches that can be applied to established teams or existing connections. Whether you're stepping into your leadership role or looking to reinvigorate your approach, the tactics I've included might serve as a helpful place for you to start. But there's one more very specific circumstance that requires a bit of extra attention and care if your goal is to create a sense of belonging within your teams…

When new hires step onto the scene (virtually or in person) for their very first interview, assignment, or visit to the office, you have an opportunity to make a crucial impact. As I mentioned a couple of chapters back, every interaction is a chance to build up, maintain, or break down relationships, and these opportunities begin to present themselves as soon as a candidate reaches out.

Right from the start, it's important to set the tone for what it means to join your team. From day one, you can shine a spotlight on your desire and determination to help all new hires adjust to a safe, comfortable environment on their journey to a sense of belonging. When new team members feel welcome and valued, they're more likely to remain engaged and motivated during their time at your organization. Here are a few of my favorite strategies to kickstart a new employee's journey to feeling they belong:

- **A warm welcome matters**. Going above and beyond right off the bat is a great way to make a good impression on your new hires. Greeting them with enthusiasm and making warm introductions to their peers can help them feel valued and appreciated. Consider hosting a welcome lunch, or introduction meeting to remind employees that a sense of belonging sometimes comes before tasks, projects, and productivity. As part of a recent strategic plan I facilitated with an agency, one of their strategic objectives feeding into developing their culture is to create a monthly New Employee Day where all new employees that month gather to learn about all the different divisions, meet possible mentors, and overall feel they belong.

- **Implement a buddy system**. Having someone to look to for help, answers, and comfort can help eliminate anxiety or loneliness during the first several weeks or months in a new role. Pairing new hires with a friendly and welcoming colleague can give people an opportunity to bond, ask questions that may feel silly or vulnerable, and get plugged into the social network in the workplace. I like to suggest short one-on-one meetings where pairs are allowed to talk about anything except for work. Another great example is a well designed and organized year long mentoring program that provides monthly question prompts for mentors and mentees to discuss, quarterly training opportunities for the mentor and mentee to attend together, goal setting sessions, and a year end celebration of completion.

- **Continue setting clear expectations**. You might be surprised to learn how beneficial it can be to help new employees create and set boundaries in their roles at work. Can you imagine how safe and valued a team member might feel after you announce to the team which tasks AREN'T their responsibility? When they feel confident in their scope of work and can acknowledge when tasks don't fall into their wheelhouse, they are much more likely to feel comfortable and valued at work. Stand up for your people, especially on their very first day.

- **Encourage open communication**. You can exemplify what it means to be authentic, approachable, and open at work and remind newcomers that they are safe to do the same. Reminding people that you are always available to talk, that feedback is always welcome, and that you are a safe space can be a great way to set the tone.

- **Recognize and celebrate individuality**. By acknowledging and celebrating the characteristics and differences that make your new hires a great fit, you can remind them - and the team - that they are valued additions to a group of diversely talented people. Doing so can help solidify their understanding and belief that differences are accepted and encouraged, creativity is valued, and their unique skills belong on the team.

- **Enable social connection and integration**. If your teams tend to gravitate towards social activities outside of the office, it may be beneficial to encourage an outing or gathering aimed at welcoming your newbies to the group. This is another great way to encourage a buddy system and bonding across departments and teams, and between colleagues. When people feel integrated into the social community, they are more likely to believe they belong.

A fellow colleague Richard Lee-Thai[11] insists that we must "Find excuses to connect. We can actively create the conditions that make meaningful connections easier. It's about finding common ground and designing the interaction in a way where it's more likely to go well."

On your journey to create a sense of belonging from day one, don't forget to lead by example. Demonstrating your own commitment to fostering a comfortable and inclusive work environment will go a long way in encouraging others to embrace and enjoy it. And isn't that the whole point?

• •

Questions to reflect upon individually, with your team, or let's connect:

1. How do you define an engaging and inclusive onboarding experience, and why is it important for the overall employee experience?

2. Can you share an example of an onboarding program that you found particularly effective, and what aspects made it stand out?

3. What strategies do you employ to create a sense of community and connection among new hires during the onboarding period?

4. How do you integrate the company's core values and culture into the onboarding experience?

5. What resources or support do you provide to help new hires navigate the organizational structure and understand their roles within the larger team?

22.

CURATING SAFE
COMMUNITY SPACES

"Everyone has a history and their own experiences.
Providing a safe environment for people to be
themselves is crucial to gaining trust,
which ultimately feeds into the success of the team."
–Mark Mostar, RN

Telling your people that work is a safe space and *actually* creating safe spaces for connection and belonging are two different things. While being vocal in your openness can go a very long way in promoting safe spaces for communities within your organization, ensuring they're implemented effectively is even better. It's the difference between merely introducing people and designating time and space for them to share and connect.

Curating safe community spaces is such a crucial part of building an environment that cultivates belonging within your organization. When you ask yourself "Where do I feel I belong?" or "Why do these places make me feel a sense of belonging?" it probably doesn't take long to realize that the people and connections you've made play a huge role. So what can we do to be a catalyst for this connection and collaboration across our own teams and organization? I asked a few experts and here's what they had to say (trust me when I say you're going to want to grab a pen):

1. "I think belonging means appreciation in a lot of ways. You have the whole aspect of teamwork and bring everyone together, making sure they all work well, but appreciation goes a long way in building that belonging and the sense of wanting to come to work and work together. Words of affirmation go a long way, whether that's somebody's love language or not, everybody likes to hear that they're doing a great job." –Amanda Gehres, Recreation Superintendent, Reynoldsburg Parks & Recreation

2. "Creating a space where people have transparency and trust debunks any myths or rumors if they believe you to be a transparent person. With that trust comes a sense of belonging. There's no reading between the lines or trying to figure things out, it makes a clear path. You don't have to wonder what they mean…you know what they mean and you believe it to be true because they value that safe space and transparent work environment." –Addie Weaver, Recreation Manager

3. "Community to me is an environment where I feel welcomed to engage. Allowing others to openly share their thoughts, feelings, and challenges creates that space for me. Making sure that my team and peers know I am open to conversations is important to me. I believe it is my communication on a regular basis, whether it is my offering to help, stopping by to say hello, or asking about how their work is going is propelling that connection and collaboration." –Jennifer Kempert, Recreation & Special Events Coordinator

Some of *my* favorite ways to encourage leaders to create safe community spaces include:

- Encouraging workplace groups (or employee resource groups (ERGs)) can enable people to build and develop their own relevant safe community spaces. ERGs might meet briefly during the workday or arrange after-hours meetups at their discretion but generally help nurture connection and inclusivity at work. A few examples of ERGs include:

    ◦ Workplace book club

    ◦ LGBTQ+ alliances

    ◦ Working parents collective

    ◦ Women's network

    ◦ Lunch and learns

    ◦ DEI initiative group

- Implementing meetings that are designated for active community discussion and personable dialogue can further establish safe spaces for your teams. Not only does it show them you're committed to holding space and time for both work- and non-work-related discussion, but it exemplifies the practice that diversity is valuable and appreciated. A few examples of designated community-focused meetings include:

    ◦ New employee check-ins with new hires from the past year

    ◦ Engage employees in your strategic planning process

    ◦ Host engaging staff development retreats

- Non-work-related lunch meetings to catch up and celebrate personal achievements

- Quarterly celebrations on progress related to your strategic plan (and maybe acknowledge a few birthdays, weddings, or other noteworthy milestones)

- Lunch and learns for creative hobbies

By simply holding space for small groups and communities at work, we're furthering the narrative that human-centric workspaces are achievable - and necessary - on the journey to achieve happier, healthier teams. Going the extra mile to create, facilitate, and encourage community and connection in safe spaces will help you achieve a sense of belonging within your organization.

• •

Questions to reflect upon individually, with your team, or let's connect:

1. How do you prioritize and curate a sense of community and safe community spaces?

2. How do you know when you've achieved a sense of safe, respectful, collaborative community?

3. What can we do to be a catalyst for this connection and collaboration?

4. What is the value of creating safe spaces and transparent relationships between individuals? How can it contribute to the larger goal of increasing a sense of belonging?

23.

MEASURING AND
IMPROVING BELONGING

"You work hard, you work together,
and you end up with a lot of friends for life."
–Michael Frisoli, aka Annie's Favorite Brother

D esigning a workplace that nurtures a sense of belonging is a big win (like, *really* big). If your goal is to retain that sense of belonging, or track your progress on your way to achieving a sense of belonging in the first place, being able to measure how people are feeling is a key factor. But how can we measure and gauge whether or not people feel they belong? It might seem like a difficult task at first, and that's a fair assumption. Measuring a sense of belonging requires trust and openness among your people. But once you've established these things (especially with some help from previous chapters), measuring belonging becomes a bit easier.

After several years of helping leaders analyze and assess their own teams to determine what might be missing, I've noted several helpful indicators and practical methods that help determine whether your people feel they belong within your work environment:

- **Take notes**. Before you try to implement any of the following approaches, create a document that will help you keep track of your current state and record progress along the way. This might look like a list of team member names with notes, a numbered scale with questions that you ask with their scores, or something else entirely. Based on the tactics that you choose to leverage, your note-taking style can be adjusted to suit your variables and team, but will ultimately help you measure and track progress over time.

- **Conduct frequent (and fun) employee surveys**. Spend some time creating a custom employee survey that addresses relevant concerns or questions for your team, and acknowledges their specific challenges, achievements, and situations. You might even choose to ask your people what they'd like to talk about in their employee surveys, and their answers can help inform your approach to checking in via survey. Keep track of their responses over time to gain a better understanding of how their sense of belonging (and other relevant data points) develops.

- **Continually collect employee feedback**. You can find "data" to help you determine how satisfied and comfortable employees feel in almost every interaction you have. No need to wait for quarterly employee surveys or team events to gather feedback and insights. Once you've created an environment that allows for open and honest communication, you'll be able to pick up on feedback during regularly scheduled meetings and discussions to help you measure a sense of belonging (among other things). Listen closely for comments about work-life balance, collaboration and connection at work, community spaces, teamwork, and an interest in exploring new skill sets to help you learn from your people and determine their levels of contentment and belonging. Interested in leveraging the entire list of thought-provoking questions that are listed throughout this book? You will find all of them at the end of the book.

- **Include employees in the decision-making process**. Do you rely on a diverse group of employees to help you make decisions and identify opportunities for your teams? Including a variety of backgrounds and experience levels in your decision-making process can help ensure that choices are made with everyone in mind, giving others an opportunity to contribute and impact your workplace culture, project goals, values, and more. Prioritizing inclusivity in the decision-making process will allow you to gather input and feedback from your people (take notes!) and prioritize their diverse needs over time.

- **Measure employee participation**. How much - or little - are your people participating in meetings, team activities, or company events? This is a great metric to track if your goal is to gain a better understanding of whether or not people feel safe, comfortable, and have a sense of belonging. A strong sense of belonging usually leads to increased engagement and a willingness to actively contribute!

- **Lean into mentorship and networking**. If you've implemented a buddy system or have other people managers on your team, check in with these mentors and leaders for the occasional temperature check. You can use their input as additional data on your journey to tracking engagement and belonging, and evaluate the success of these mentorship programs within your teams. Not only do these connections help employees collaborate, they also contribute to a better sense of belonging.

When I asked some of my fellow leaders how they manage to track and monitor engagement levels and a sense of belonging across their teams, here's what they had to say:

1. "Daily communications with peers and staff are how I measure my belonging. I learn who I am more comfortable speaking to and when I should approach an individual with conflict. Belonging is how I measure my importance and leadership among my team. Can I easily be replaced? Or am I irreplaceable?" –Jennifer Kempert, Recreation & Special Events Coordinator

2. "We know from research that love and belonging are basic needs - right after survival needs like food, shelter, and clothing. I ask people how they feel about the team as a whole and their spot on the team. I can try to gauge it all I want, but directly asking is the easiest and fastest way to get the answer. Plus, people feel valued and respected when they're asked important questions like this!" –Judd Walker, Director of Student Leadership, Ohio University

3. "If everyone on the team feels they are treated the same, then the sense of belonging within the team will happen automatically. My team sees each other as a family because of the dynamic that we have together." –Sequellia Logan, Deputy Administrator/Athletics

. . . .

Questions to reflect upon individually, with your team, or let's connect:

1. How do you define a sense of belonging within the workplace, and why is it important for employee engagement and satisfaction?

2. How do you attempt to measure a sense of belonging within your teams? What is the value of collecting this information, and what can/do you do with it?

3. Can you share an example of a successful initiative or program that positively impacted employees' sense of belonging, and how did you measure its success?

4. How do you measure the impact of leadership behavior and communication on employees' sense of belonging?

5. In what ways do you involve employees in the co-creation of initiatives aimed at enhancing a sense of belonging?

24.

LET THEM SPEAK

*"My enjoyment as a leader comes
from watching others create."*
—Patrick Hammer, Director of Parks and Recreation, Town of Erie

So much of the advice throughout the past four sections of this book aims to help you facilitate or harness the power of feedback and employee contributions. Hopefully, this helps you create a more enjoyable, productive, thriving workplace. But perhaps the most crucial component of progress at work is the willingness of your people to contribute. Without an open, safe, approachable, comfortable environment and an eagerness on their behalf to participate, very little change can happen.

In an article about improving workplace culture through compassion[12], the Center for Creative Leadership shares, "Ultimately, compassionate leadership changes an entire organization's culture, yielding greater cooperation and grace for all. Employees trust their leaders and each other, giving others the benefit of the doubt. As a result, senior leaders feel more comfortable taking bold, courageous actions. And when their people feel heard and sense that their perspectives and experiences are valued, they're better able to support those bold actions, which benefits the entire enterprise."

Creating space to let them speak and thrive is critical, and thankfully, achievable through the right tactics and a compassionate, thoughtful approach. As we attempt to design workplaces and company cultures that contribute to our organization-wide missions and enable employees to thrive both within and beyond work, an open dialogue is one of the best ways I can think of to help us get there.

Usually, a team is made up of a variety of individuals and personalities. Some are outgoing and confident, others are shy or reserved, some are humorous, others are serious, a few may be generous while others focus studiously on their own tasks. This variety and diversity ultimately result in a culture where some feel incredibly comfortable sharing and contributing, and others need a bit more encouragement.

Additionally, beyond one's willingness to contribute, we must recognize the frequency of opportunities they have to do so. The more opportunities our people have to participate safely, the more we can run with this input and create tangible change within our organizations.

When people feel more connected to you as a leader, the environment you've created, and the organization in which you operate, they are far more likely to share ideas, make contributions, provide honest feedback, and be upfront about concerns. This is why it's so important to create and leave space for our people to speak up.

As leaders, we sometimes feel like we have to fill the space, have an answer to every question, and have ideas to help solve any obstacle that arises. Sometimes we might even feel like it's our job to show off our knowledge or insights. The truth is that listening, allowing space to exist, and creating more opportunities for others to share personal and professional insights is actually what creates a deeper sense of belonging, and results in richer contributions from everyone.

Since it can be really difficult to hold back from contributing or allow others to take up space and share ideas, I asked my network to share their best tips and insights.

1. "As you grow in your role as a leader, you learn that your capacity is limited, and you have to lead *others* to be contributors. There can be discomfort in others' approach to problem-solving or program delivery. But you have to remember, they're never going to get good at it unless you allow them to have the same ups and downs and trials and tribulations and opportunities to grow and develop [that you did]. If we constantly insert ourselves in the minutia of getting to the bigger goal, we shortcut not only what could be good for the organization, but we shortcut their development and we shortcut the future leaders of the organization." –Stacie Anaya, Director

2. "I realize I am doing too much [problem-solving] when my team keeps coming back to me for decisions, tasks, and challenges. I don't want to be a crutch as a leader and I want them to feel *they* are the experts. I try to remember to ask developmental questions like "What is your gut telling you to do with this situation?" or "What is your heart telling you?"- In addition, our employee engagement surveys say people want to feel empowered, so I need to encourage opportunities to make them feel empowered. Asking developmental questions and *listening more* helps employees hone in on their critical thinking skills, and helps develop them for more strategic roles." –Rosemary Richmond, Director of Customer Success

3. "When leaders speak and lead the conversation, subordinates often feel like what they have to say isn't important. One of the best things a leader can do is listen to their team." –Nancy Pfeffer,

Regional Manager, CPP, The Maryland - National Capital Park and Planning Commission

Recognizing the importance of holding back is half the battle. Creating platforms and safe spaces for others to contribute is the perfect next step. I also asked a few of my connections to share tangible ways that they create space and a safe environment for others to speak up and share at work, and here's what they had to say:

1. "As hard as it is, [you have to allow] people to fail. I don't like this because it's a little bit of a control issue for me, but I know it's important because I've been there – and I want others to grow, too. I vividly remember my first couple of moments of failure in the field. But I can also remember how much I learned from those moments. I want to ensure that people are failing gracefully, and remind myself that when I allow for failure and learning to occur, it's actually for the longevity of knowledge for the individual." –Amanda Gehres, Recreation Superintendent, Reynoldsburg Parks & Recreation

2. "I meet with my team as a whole monthly and have every staff member contribute to the meeting - whether professionally or personally. I also let staff and other employees know that my door is always open and have had amazing conversations with staff who do not report to me cause they feel safe. My staff knows that they can have harder conversations with me in private and I tell them that I will never embarrass them in front of others and that any conversations meant to be private will stay private." –Chris Webber, CPRP, Superintendent of Finance & Personnel

3. "We believe in "Psychological Safety", where team members have the freedom to give and receive feedback, raise issues or concerns,

disagree, ask difficult decisions, and admit errors all without having a fear of repercussions." –Kenny Patterson, Sr. Director - Implementation, Sunland Logistics Solutions

When I reflect on the previous two dozen chapters included in this book, I can't help but recognize just how much these insights and sentiments reinforce my belief that *people are our superpower*. As our greatest asset, it's our job to protect, nurture, and encourage our people as best we can to strengthen our sense of community, inspire growth, and design belonging both in the workplace and in the world.

It's almost as if I saved the best (and most important) sentiment for last because making space for others is how we make space for growth, change, purpose, meaning, inspiration, celebration, and peace. On your journey to be a better leader and foster a deeper sense of belonging, keep in mind that your people are your greatest asset, and the care and compassion you show them can truly change the world.

• •

Questions to reflect upon individually, with your team, or let's connect:

1. How do you create space for your team members to share thoughts and ideas, or foster an environment that feels safe to do so?

2. Why is it so important, as leaders, to hold back from contributing sometimes, and instead, allow your people to take up space and share ideas? What is the benefit of encouraging them to speak freely?

3. What strategies do you employ to ensure that quieter or introverted team members have an opportunity to speak up during meetings or discussions?

4. In what ways do you actively seek out and value diverse perspectives when making decisions or solving problems within the team?

5. How do you model open communication as a leader, and what steps do you take to continually reinforce the importance of everyone's voice within the team?

GO FORTH AND INSPIRE

I nspiring growth by designing belonging requires intentionality, consideration, and an openness to surprise. In fact, if you had told me a few years back that someday I'd attempt to compile all of my highest-impact insights into a book, I might've looked at you funny for just a moment before resigning to the fact that life is more fun when you embrace this element of surprise. So, while I'm not *totally* shocked that my journey so far has led me to this point, I am incredibly eager to share it with my community in hopes that it ignites the spark inside anyone who needs it.

While it's impossible to effectively summarize the tips and knowledge that I included throughout the rest of this book, I would regret not telling you that sometimes, embracing the concept of Leadership by Design *is* as simple as stopping to smell the roses. My career is freckled with moments of immense gratitude and acknowledgment for the gift of leading others, being led by others, and everything in between. Pausing to reflect on how far you've come, how large your community has grown, how supported you are by your "village," and the long list of opportunities - known or unknown - that lie ahead is one of the best ways to remain intentional and energetic throughout your career (and life in general). In fact, many of life's greatest and most fruitful surprises happen when you take the time to let them show up.

As you move forward through your intentional leadership journey, some of the most important reminders to keep in mind are those that help you remain grounded in your own values while simultaneously supporting others and their values, too.

You don't have to start with everything, all at once (hello, burnout!), but instead, choose a few areas that feel applicable to you and your own teams, and start there. Have patience and be kind to yourself as you attempt to embrace new approaches, sharpen new skill sets, and center yourself around new or improved values. Success won't happen overnight, but it will make itself known through the small, quiet moments of improvement and growth. Blink and you might miss it, so be sure to keep your gratitude goggles on as much as possible.

Lastly, as you embrace all that falls under the umbrella of "Leadership by Design," continue to remind yourself just how spectacular you are. People are our superpower, and that includes you, too. As we embark on a path that often requires enthusiasm and excitement for others, it can be easy to forget that we are deserving of these same celebrations. Find something - no matter how small - to celebrate each day and lead yourself, first.

AUTHOR'S NOTE

As I pen the final words of this book while reflecting on my leadership journey as a whole, I'm filled with immense gratitude for the incredible community of people who cheer me on at every turn. It's often said that leadership is not a solo act, and I am so proud to be able to attest to the profound truth of this statement. I owe the completion of this book, and my growth as a human and leader, to the remarkable network of people who have shown up as my unwavering pillars of support.

I also want to express my heartfelt gratitude to my family and friends - my personal network and support system of loved ones - who continue to stand by me with unwavering support and love. Your belief in me has been a constant source of courage, strength, and motivation. You've provided me with the emotional sustenance that has fueled my journey as a wife, daughter, sibling, friend, leader, and now...author.

First and foremost, thank you to my nearest and dearest who continue to support me relentlessly. Thank you to my husband Kenny, to put it simply, without you none of this is possible. Thank you for your love, inspiration, acceptance, listening, brainstorming, tech support/HR support/administrative support/operations support, laughter, team mentality, and go for it attitude. No words can capture the gratitude I have for you and our life together. Thank you to my cheerleader parents, your belief in me *throughout life* has been a constant source of courage, strength, and motivation. Thank you to my enthusiastic siblings, my energizing cousins, and two of the very best friends to exist, your laughs, listening, and encouragement have been such a gift. My love and appreciation for all of you and all that you do is profound.

Next, I am honored to extend my deepest appreciation to my professional network - the mentors, colleagues, and collaborators who have shared their wisdom, experiences, and knowledge with me throughout the years. Your insights have enriched the chapters throughout this book and, most importantly, have strengthened my understanding of what it means to be a leader. Your invaluable encouragement and guidance leave me feeling incredibly fortunate to have such a remarkable group of professionals in my corner.

Lastly, thank you to my writer Savannah Benavides, whose expertise allowed me to proudly carry this book across the finish line. As the owner of Copy Compass (you can visit *yourcopycompass.com* to learn more about Savannah and explore her services or writing resources), she brought clarity and skill to this project. From the beginning, she understood and connected with my vision, and together, we transformed my ideas into a polished and cohesive story. I am grateful for her commitment and the contributions she made to this book. Savannah, you are a true wordsmith, and this book's success is a reflection of your talent and unwavering support. Thank you for helping bring my ideas to life.

Leadership, as I've come to understand, is not a solitary pursuit. It's a collaborative, creative, constantly changing effort born from the collective wisdom and strength of a team. I'm blessed to have had not one, but two incredible teams - one in my professional life, and the other in my personal life. I'm even luckier to have several people in my life who show up fiercely for both teams as needed. Your support and guidance have made this book possible, all while shaping the leader that I am today.

As your journey through this book comes to an end, I hope you find inspiration, insights, and a renewed sense of purpose in your own leadership journey. Remember, no matter where you are in life, you'll always have a team to rely on.

With appreciation and a heart full of gratitude,

Annie Frisoli
Founder & CEO
Creating Community LLC`

THANK YOU TO MY NETWORK

This book wouldn't be nearly as powerful if it weren't for the incredible people willing to contribute their perspectives, insights, and advice. Thank you to my network of resilient, influential, graceful, and kind humans who took the time to share their thoughts with me for this project. Your contributions helped me grow, and through this book, will go on to help others grow, too.

- Stacie Anaya, Director

- Bernita, Director

- Steven Carter, Deputy Director, Maryland-National Park/Planning Commission

- Amy Dingle, Director of Outdoor Connections, Five Rivers MetroParks

- Bryan Dixon, Deputy Director, Park Services, Henry County Parks and Recreation

- Amanda Gehres, Recreation Superintendent, Reynoldsburg Parks & Recreation

- Miranda Gomez, Community Services Director, City of Buckeye

- Nicolette Griese, Assistant Director - Student Involvement Center, Fort Lewis College

- Kevin Grothe, Vice President of Sponsorships, Memphis in May International Festival

- Patrick Hammer, Director of Parks & Recreation, Town of Erie

- K D Howell-EL, Recreation Center Director

- Jennifer Kempert, Recreation & Special Events Coordinator

- Maria C. Klein, Art Department Coordinator

- Dianna Lawrence, Superintendent of Community Events, City of Richardson

- Sequellia Logan, Deputy Administrator/Athletics

- Johan Moerman, Board Member & Advisor in the Festival and Cultural Industries, Former CEO of Rotterdam Festivals

- Mark Mostar, RN

- Nathan Musteen, Director - Parks & Recreation, City of Raymore

- Manny Padia, Recreation Administrator

- Lisa Paradis, Consultant, BerryDunn

- Kenny Patterson, Sr. Director - Implementation, Sunland Logistics Solutions

- Erica Perez, Recreation Manager

- Mairin Petrone, Executive Director, Pittsburgh Irish Festival

- Nancy Pfeffer, Regional Manager, CPRP, The Maryland - National Capital Park and Planning Commission

- Rosemary Richmond, Director of Customer Success

- Stuart Schleien, Professor Emeritus, UNC Greensboro

- Chad Snow, Chief Operating Officer, BerryDunn

- Judd Walker, Director of Student Leadership, Ohio University

- Addie Weaver, Recreation Manager

- Chris Webber, CPRP, Superintendent of Finance & Personnel

- Trevor Welcher, Parks & Recreation Director

SOURCES AND CITATIONS

1. Center for Creative Leadership. "How to Boost Employee Engagement and Motivation." https://www.ccl.org/articles/leading-effectively-articles/3-ways-to-boost-employee-motivation/.

2. Center for Creative Leadership. "Direction, Alignment, and Commitment Assessment." 9 March 2019, https://www.ccl.org/insights-research/direction-alignment-and-commitment-assessment

3. Soren Kaplan. "Invisible Advantage Book & Toolkit - Culture of Innovation." https://www.sorenkaplan.com/invisibleadvantage/

4. Iracki, Anthony. "LET'S TURN "WE'VE TRIED THAT BEFORE" INTO "LET'S TRY THAT AGAIN."" Anthony in Parks, 2 October 2022, https://anthonyinparks.com/blog/f/turnweve-already-tried-that-into-lets-try-that-again

5. Black, Mark. The Resilience Roadmap: 7 Guideposts for Charting Your Course in a Chaotic World.

6. IDEO U. "How to Use Data for Innovation – IDEO U." *IDEO U*, https://www.ideou.com/blogs/inspiration/how-to-use-data-for-innovation

7. Center for Creative Leadership. "How to Succeed at Complex, Continuous Change." https://www.ccl.org/articles/leading-effectively-articles/succeed-complex-continuous-change/

8. Harvard Business Review. "To Lead, Create a Shared Vision." Harvard Business Review, January 2009, https://hbr.org/2009/01/to-lead-create-a-shared-vision

9. Watkinson, Allan, and Rohit Kar. "Organizational Culture: What Leaders Need to Know." Gallup, 24 March 2023, https://www.gallup.com/workplace/471968/culture-transformation-leaders-needknow.aspx?utm_source=workplace&utm_medium=email&utm_campaign=culture_audit_email_2_august_08232023&utm_term=nurture&utm_content=leaders_existing_culture_and_the_one_they_aspire_to_

10. Fly, Blake. Blake Fly - Speaker And Business Coach For Family-Oriented Entrepreneurs, https://blakefly.com/

11. Lee-Thai, Richard. Excuses to Connect, https://excusestoconnect.com/

12. Center for Creative Leadership. "Better Culture Starts With Compassionate Leadership" 10 February 2023, https://www.ccl.org/articles/leading-effectively-articles/create-better-culture-start-with-compassionate-leadership/